Sport in Iceland

T0383702

Iceland is a tiny Nordic nation with a population of just 330,000 and no professional sports leagues, and yet its soccer, basketball and handball teams have all qualified for major international tournaments in recent years. This fascinating study argues that team sport success is culturally produced and that in order to understand collective achievement we have to consider the socio-cultural context.

Based on unparalleled access to key personnel, including top coaches, athletes and administrators, the book explores Icelandic cultural capital as a factor in sporting success, from traditions of workmanship, competitive play and teamwork to international labor migration and knowledge transfer. The first book to focus specifically on the socio-cultural aspects of a small nation's international sporting success, this is an original and illuminating contribution to the study of the sociology of sport.

Sport in Iceland: How Small Nations Achieve International Success is fascinating reading for team sport enthusiasts, coaches, managers and organisers, as well as for any student or scholar with an interest in the sociology of sport, strategic sports development, sports policy or sports administration.

Vidar Halldorsson is an assistant professor in sociology at the University of Iceland.

Routledge Focus on Sport, Culture and Society

Routledge Focus on Sport, Culture and Society showcases the latest cutting-edge research in the sociology of sport and exercise. Concise in form (20,000–50,000 words) and published quickly (within three months), the books in this series represents an important channel through which authors can disseminate their research swiftly and make an impact on current debates. We welcome submissions on any topic within the socio-cultural study of sport and exercise, including but not limited to subjects such as gender, race, sexuality, disability, politics, the media, social theory, Olympic Studies, and the ethics and philosophy of sport. The series aims to be theoretically-informed, empirically-grounded and international in reach, and will include a diversity of methodological approaches.

Available in this series:

Sport in Iceland
How Small Nations Achieve International Success
Vidar Halldorsson

Sport in Iceland

How Small Nations Achieve
International Success

Vidar Halldorsson

Routledge
Taylor & Francis Group

LONDON AND NEW YORK

First published 2017 by Routledge

2 Park Square, Milton Park, Abingdon, Oxfordshire OX14 4RN
52 Vanderbilt Avenue, New York, NY 10017

Routledge is an imprint of the Taylor & Francis Group, an informa business

First issued in paperback 2019

British Library Cataloguing-in-Publication Data
A catalogue record for this book is available from the British Library

Library of Congress Cataloging-in-Publication Data
A catalog record for this book has been requested

ISBN: 978-1-138-68179-8 (hbk)
ISBN: 978-0-367-34502-0 (pbk)

Typeset in Times New Roman
by Apex CoVantage, LLC

To Þórólfur Þórlindsson

Contents

Preface
"The general within the particular"

The sociological literature has not addressed sporting achievement to any extent; this has been left to other disciplines such as sports psychology, physiology and even business. Nor has it been the custom for sporting organizations and sports teams to seek the help of sociologists in order to help lay the foundations of a successful sporting culture, aimed at high-level sporting achievement, or to help sports teams achieve their potential in competition.

For some years now, my professional activity has embraced my academic career as a sociologist – doing research on the social aspects of sporting performance – and work as a practicing sports consultant in Iceland – helping sports organizations and teams to lay the foundations of sporting success. Owing to my experience in these fields I am inclined to approach sporting achievement from a socio-cultural perspective at the collective level instead of, as is customary, at the individual-level. My perspective is grounded in the idea that all sporting achievement is built on collective action and can therefore be viewed as cultural productions that are informed by traditions, norms and values.

In this book I will try to present the case of collective sporting achievement as a cultural production by analyzing the recent and intriguing sporting successes of the various national sports teams of Iceland. My main task is to locate, what Gary Alan Fine (2012) phrased as "the general within the particular"; that is, to show how elements that reside in the general culture are represented in how sports teams perform in action. Thus, the underlying argument in this book is that the discipline of sociology can make an important contribution in helping to fill a gap in our understanding of collective sporting achievements.

Howard S. Becker ([1982]/2008) argues that all social action is collective in nature. This book is no exception, and I want to thank those who helped me, in one way or the other, along the way. First, I want to acknowledge my debt to my mentor, Þórólfur Þórlindsson, for his guidance, support and enthusiasm for our sociological work, as well as our friendship, in the last 20 years. Many of the concepts and ideas proposed in this book are the harvest of our discussions and collaboration through the years. I should like to express special gratitude to Michael A. Katovich, Stephen G. Wieting and Jón Gunnar Bernburg for their valuable help with the manuscript, and to Jeffrey Cosser for helping me improve the language of this book. I want to thank the University of Iceland Research fund; Aron Gauti Kristjánsson and Signý Rún Jóhannesdóttir, for their assistance with the interviews; Gísli Pálsson, Inga Dóra Sigfúsdóttir, Stefán Hrafn Jónsson, Arnar Eggert Thoroddsen, Baldur Þórhallsson, Ragna Benedikta Garðarsdóttir, Guðni Th. Jóhannesson, Gunnar Valgeirsson and Frode Telseth for their invaluable comments and assistance. I further want to thank the interviewees who gave their time and shared their insights into the sporting world, which provided me with the "rich" material that I had for this book. Finally, I want to thank my wife Ásdís, our kids and our families for their support and simply for "being there." *Huh!*

References

Becker, H.S. ([1982]/2008). *Art worlds*. Berkeley: University of California Press.
Fine, G.H. (2012). *Tiny publics: A theory of group action and culture*. New York: Russell Sage Foundation.

Part I

Setting the scene

1 Introduction
"Small" teams and "big" results

I call it the Icelandic miracle.

– Ramón Calderón[1]

On 28 June 2016, Iceland beat England 2–1 in the pre-quarter-finals in the European Men's Football Championship. This victory eliminated England from the competition and placed Iceland in the quarter-finals against the hosts, France. The result was a shock to the football world. How could such a tiny nation – with an amateur football league and a joint-coach who works part-time as a dentist – eliminate England – the birthplace of football with one of the most prestigious football leagues in the world?

The unexpected result attracted worldwide attention. Searches for Iceland on the Google search engine multiplied during the competition – reaching the same level as when an Icelandic volcano, Eyjafjallajökull, erupted and disrupted all air traffic in Europe in 2010.[2] However, the results of this single match not only evoked such attention (surprise results tend to happen in sports), but the fact that such a small nation qualified for and reached the quarter-finals in one of the largest sporting competitions in the world's most popular sport came as a shock to followers of the sport. Reporters from all over the world traveled to this tiny island to cover the story of the national football team. What secret did Icelandic football keep?

Modern sports emphasize winning, and what makes a winning team is a sort of Holy Grail in modern sports (Cashmore, 2002). This goal to win is also the case in business or anywhere else where the result stems from cooperation between individuals striving towards a common goal. But winning usually belongs to those with the most resources. At the end of the day, especially in sports, the biggest, strongest and richest usually win. The professionalization and commercialization of modern sports, in the late twentieth century, have further widened the gap, in terms of financial resources, between the levels of "those who have" and "those who have not." A deep divide between the richest and the rest exists and has become ingrained into the system. Thus, the top spots in modern elite sports are dominated by the most resourceful and the wealthiest.

An ideal team composed from a variety of important resources would probably be very successful, but there can be no certainty of such an outcome. Sports history constantly reminds us that results are unpredictable and, despite predictability based on wealth and resources, there is no guarantee of success. This uncertainty is especially the case in team sports where, in theory, the best players should make the best team. But in practice, there is no certainty that the team with the best players, with the most money, or with the highest status will win. The world of sports regularly witnesses unforeseen results and remarkable achievements of the "underdogs." The occasional "Cinderella stories" tell tales of great achievements and victories by the underdogs that are against all odds. While two opposing teams have the same number of players on the field and play by the same rules, the individual game has features of its own and intrinsic dynamics that cannot be determined beforehand. The uncertainty of the outcome is a fundamental element of modern competitive sport, which preserves the ongoing popularity of sports and further motivates those with smaller resources to keep on trying because they have seen that anything can happen. These facts make sporting success such an intriguing phenomenon.

Thus, sports are not only systematic and mechanical – elements that have been highlighted by the increased professionalization of sport – but they also contain something that is unknowable. Sports are based on collective action, and they even tend to be colored by extraneous associations, such as team or national identity. Asking any sports fan proves this point. Such examples further imply that the mechanical, calculated and professional approach to sport – as is customary in the commercialized and professional world of modern sports – falls short of being a winning formula in sporting contests. Team success consists of something more than the paid-for sum of the team's valuable parts. Thus, there seem to be other dynamics at play in team sports apart from those which professional sports have already fully utilized. This book is about such a "Cinderella story," a story some have referred to as "the miracle" that is the case of Iceland's national sports teams.

The case of Iceland

As mentioned, the sporting success of Iceland – a tiny Nordic nation with a population of 330,000 – has attracted widespread international attention[3] (see further Kuper and Szimansky, 2014; Wieting, 2015). This success was highlighted when the Icelandic men's national team qualified for the UEFA European Championship finals in 2015, where, as one of the 16 remaining teams, it beat England and reached the quarter-finals stage. Iceland's football success has spurred a flow of interest as to how such a tiny nation could achieve such a result, surpassing the goals of much larger and more prestigious sporting nations. But the achievement of Iceland's men's football team is just the tip of the iceberg – a fact that surprises the international sports world, which has predominantly focused on men's football. It has become a general trend for the Icelandic national teams to punch above their weight at the international level in all major team sports played in the country, such as football, handball, basketball and team gymnastics. The achievements of Iceland's teams far surpass the perceived probability of success for such a small nation. The Icelandic teams involved have written their names in the history books of major international team sports competitions, not only by participating, but also by winning medals in these contests. These results include an Olympic team medal and European championship medals, in addition to qualifying for major international tournaments, which is often described as a major accomplishment for such a small nation. Interestingly, the achievements of all but one of these Icelandic national teams, the men's handball team, have occurred in the last decade, a period that may be termed as a "golden age" of Icelandic sports.

As a tiny nation, Iceland is sometimes referred to as a micro-state (Sam, 2016). The population of Wales is 10 times larger than Iceland's, Denmark's is 17 times larger and England's population is over 150 times larger. In population, the whole of Iceland is similar to single cities such as Coventry, Düsseldorf or Utrecht. This small population poses a great challenge for Icelandic teams in international sports: the national teams have a much smaller pool of athletes to draw on than larger nations, putting Iceland at a serious disadvantage at the outset. It can be very difficult for a tiny population to produce players for national teams with the talent or the right physical attributes for certain sports. This difficulty becomes apparent in sports such as basketball and handball, where the Icelandic teams have shorter players than most of their opponents (see Chapter 6): at any given time, a small population simply has limited numbers of players with the right physical attributes for specific sports. Iceland's success despite a small talent pool is therefore a considerable achievement for a tiny nation. While simply qualifying for major sport tournaments is an achievement in itself for Iceland, winning medals at such tournaments exceeds even optimistic expectations. In the last decade Iceland has managed to do both, and in different team sports.

One sport in particular that stands out, team handball, demonstrates the extent to which Iceland has excelled. Historically, going back to the 1950s, Iceland has had a long and successful tradition in men's team handball (Thorlindsson and Halldorsson, 2017). Until 2008 no other Icelandic national team qualified for a major championship (see Table 1.1). The

Table 1.1 Overview of participation and results of the Icelandic teams in major international tournaments in Iceland's most popular team sports, 1958–2017

Year	Sport	Team	Competition	Results
1958	Handball	Men	World Championship Finals	9th place
1961	Handball	Men	World Championship Finals	6th place
1964	Handball	Men	World Championship Finals	9th place
1970	Handball	Men	World Championship Finals	11th place
1972	Handball	Men	Olympic Games	12th place
1974	Handball	Men	World Championship Finals	14th place
1978	Handball	Men	World Championship Finals	13th place
1984	Handball	Men	Olympic Games	6th place
1986	Handball	Men	World Championship Finals	6th place
1988	Handball	Men	Olympic Games	8th place
1990	Handball	Men	World Championship Finals	10th place
1992	Handball	Men	Olympic Games	4th place
1993	Handball	Men	World Championship Finals	8th place
1995	Handball	Men	World Championship Finals	14th place
1997	Handball	Men	World Championship Finals	5th place
2000	Handball	Men	European Championship Finals	11th place
2001	Handball	Men	World Championship Finals	11th place
2002	Handball	Men	European Championship Finals	4th place
2003	Handball	Men	World Championship Finals	7th place
2004	Handball	Men	European Championship Finals	13th place
2004	Handball	Men	Olympic Games	9th place
2005	Handball	Men	World Championship Finals	15th place
2006	Handball	Men	European Championship Finals	7th place
2007	Handball	Men	World Championship Finals	8th place
2008	Handball	Men	European Championship Finals	11th place
2008	Handball	Men	Olympic Games	Silver medal
2009	Football	Women	European Championship Finals	Group stage
2010	Handball	Men	European Championship Finals	Bronze medal
2010	Handball	Women	European Championship Finals	15th place
2011	Handball	Men	World Championship Finals	6th place
2011	Handball	Women	World Championship Finals	12th place
2012	Handball	Men	European Championship Finals	10th place
2012	Handball	Women	European Championship Finals	15th place
2012	Handball	Men	Olympic Games	5th place
2013	Handball	Men	World Championship Finals	12th place
2013	Football	Women	European Championship Finals	Quarter-finals
2014	Handball	Men	European Championship Finals	5th place
2015	Handball	Men	World Championship Finals	11th place
2015	Basketball	Men	European Championship Finals	24th place
2016	Handball	Men	European Championship Finals	16th place
2016	Football	Men	European Championship Finals	Quarter-finals
2017	Handball	Men	World Championship Finals	N/A
2017	Football	Women	European Championship Finals	N/A
2017	Basketball	Men	European Championship Finals	N/A

men's handball team has earned a significant status in the world of international handball where, in 2013, it was placed fifth in the world, according to an unofficial ranking list.[4] Icelandic coaches also enjoy high prestige in international handball where they coach some of the best club teams in the world, as well as some of the top national teams such as those of the men's 2015 European champions, Germany; 2016 Olympic champions, Denmark; and the women's 2015 world champions, Norway.

The men's handball team had on several occasions come close to winning a medal at a major championship (see Steinarsson, 1994) but it wasn't until 2008 – half a century after its first qualification for a major championship – that the team won its first major team medal:[5] a silver at the Olympic Games in Beijing. A few weeks later the women's football team made its breakthrough when it qualified for the European Championship finals, becoming only the second Icelandic national team to do so (beside the men's handball team). From then on, the floodgates have opened, with the Icelandic national teams in women's handball, and in men's basketball and football, all qualifying for major international tournaments. The only team not to do so, of the three major Icelandic team sports, is the women's basketball team. Moreover, the women's gymnastics team won the European Championship in 2010 and 2013. In total, Icelandic national teams have managed to qualify 44 times for major international tournaments and almost half of these occasions (N=20) have been since 2008.

The leap of Iceland's football teams in the ranking tables in recent years is striking. In 2010 the men's team was ranked 133rd in the FIFA world ranking. In 2016 the team achieved its highest ranking in history, 21st, making Iceland the highest-ranked Nordic nation.[6] The women's team has been rather more stable over the last years at around 15th place in the FIFA world rankings. Interestingly, only four nations ended in the quarter-finals in the last European football finals in both men's and women's competitions: Germany, France, Italy and Iceland. Eyjólfsson has argued that Iceland was one of the top eight European football nations in 2016.[7]

When compared to that of other micro-states in Europe, or states with small populations, Iceland's team-sport success is unique. While bigger nations in somewhat similar size category (such as Cyprus, Montenegro, Luxemburg and Malta) have collectively only a handful of qualifications for major team sport tournaments, Iceland has managed to qualify on 44 occasions for major tournaments, in three sports, putting it in a league of its own among the micro-states of Europe. Comparing Iceland to other countries with relatively small populations indicates that the consistency of the achievements of the various Icelandic national teams in the past decade cannot be dismissed as flukes. Nowadays, Icelanders expect their national teams will be competing with the best in the world; it could be said that Icelanders will not settle for less.

Against all odds

The achievements described above are not only interesting in the light of the small population of Iceland. They are intriguing in several ways. First, why did all those Icelandic teams arrive at the top international level at the same time? Up until 2008, only the men's handball team had managed to qualify for a major international tournament; since then, however, the men's and women's football teams, the women's handball team and the men's basketball team have all managed to do the same.

Second, Iceland has, in recent years, managed to reach the top level in several team sports, but to a much lesser extent in individual sports. Yet the chances of competing at the highest level in individual sports should be greater for a small nation. Small nations should be more able to produce one top-level athlete than to supply an entire corpus of top-level athletes at any given time; however, in recent years Iceland has not produced individual stars at the Olympic Games. Since its first participation in 1908, it has only won three medals in individual sports at the Games. Wieting (2015) has pointed out that Icelanders have been overly successful in periphery sports that are based on strength. Icelandic men have been successful in the strongmen contests, as have Icelandic women in the international CrossFit contests. Although in recent years Iceland has seen some important steps in the restoration of high achievements in traditional Icelandic individual sports, especially in swimming and track and field, it can be argued that Icelandic national teams have been more successful at the international level since the turn of the century than have individual athletes from Iceland. This trend is illustrated by the fact that no individual sport athlete won the Icelandic Sportsperson of the Year award from 2001 until 2015.[8] This disparity in success indicates that its achievements are collective in nature.

Third, it can be argued that although the Icelandic teams have done exceptionally well in international competitions, they do not necessarily consist of world-class athletes. This lack of world-class designation has been the case in all the aforementioned teams – with the possible exception of the men's handball team, which has had world-class players who play with some of the best teams in the world and regularly play in the Champions League finals. Members of the other teams do not play with the best teams in the world. For instance, only a handful of Icelandic football players have played at the highest professional level in club team football (i.e., the Champions League), and only one of them, Eiður Smári Guðjohnsen, was in a team that qualified from the group stages when, in 2009, his team, FC Barcelona, won the league title. Only one Icelandic basketball player, Pétur Guðmundsson, has played in the NBA: he played for the

Portland Trailblazers, LA Lakers and San Antonio Spurs in the 1980s. Only a handful of the Icelandic national players in all sports, beside handball, play in the top leagues in the world; most play in Scandinavia and Western Europe or in lower leagues in the big countries. Thus, the achievements of the Icelandic national teams cannot be explained by arguing that the teams are built around super-talented individual athletes – Ronaldos or Zlatans – who take their teams up to higher levels.

Fourth, the amateur sport system in Iceland is based on voluntary movements and the ethos of amateur sports. Financially, Icelandic sports, especially elite sports, do not compare favorably to elite sports in other Western nations. Iceland does not maintain the infrastructure, systematic approaches or scientific methods that exist in the professional world of sports; such dynamics have been identified as important for other nations that have excelled in sports (Beamish and Ritchie, 2006; Bloomfield, 2003; Epstein, 2013; Hill, 2007).

Finally, Iceland's success cannot be explained be specific sport hegemony. It can be argued that nations can succeed in an activity if they prioritize it and put more resources into it than into other alternatives; sometimes this is referred to as "putting all eggs in the same basket." Foreigners who have analyzed the successful handball tradition in Iceland have assumed that the sport occupies a hegemonic status as not only the main sport in Iceland but also the key sport in the national consciousness. But such a status has not become evident. Handball is only one of the sports that Icelanders play, and neither the most popular nor the most prestigious. Foreigners are surprised when they are told that handball is not a key subject in the school curriculum in Iceland, along with math and Icelandic.[9] Multi-sports are emphasized in Iceland and its national teams have been doing well in several sports at the same time. It could be argued that the achievements of Iceland's national sports teams were epitomized in 2014 and 2015 when the men's football, basketball and handball teams all qualified for the European Championship finals at the same time. It is generally thought that for small nations it is a tall order to build one top-level sport team at any given time, but to do so in three major team sports simultaneously – from the same generation of athletes – is unprecedented for such a small nation.

The achievements of the Icelandic teams defy probabilities and conventional expectations and pose the question of how such a tiny nation can accomplish such results – in many sports at the same time – exceeding accomplishments of larger and prestigious sporting nations? All the above-mentioned arguments suggest that the sporting achievements of the Icelandic national teams were not based on the conventional assumptions in such cases, such as those regarding individual talents or specific sports technicalities. In effect, one key argument of this book is that a national sporting success, such as Iceland's, is a cultural product, as me and my colleague have argued elsewhere in these words:

> The sociological study of achievement should not be confined to the study of individual characteristics. One world class athlete or one world class team may raise interesting questions about the role of socialization and the social environment in the production of sport success, but it does not make for an interesting social phenomenon or a central sociological topic. The emergence of a large group of world-class athletes, coaches and strong national teams that continue to come from a confined geographical area constitute a social tradition, which is a topic for a sociological inquiry.
>
> (Thorlindsson and Halldorsson, 2017)

All sports are built on social action, which is dynamic and not the result of neat and linear relationships (see Becker, 2007). Applying simple cause-and-effect analysis leaves researchers with major shortcomings in understanding the dynamic nature of a nation's collective sporting achievement. The aim of this book is to analyze national sporting success of a tiny nation from a socio-cultural perspective by looking at the achievements of the Icelandic national teams in football, handball, basketball and team gymnastics.

This book

I have examined the general assumption, which at first glance would seem the intuitively correct conclusion, that high-level performance in team sports is automatically the preserve of large nations; that is, those having a large pool of athletes to choose from for their national teams. However, the success of Iceland's men's team in the European Football Championship in 2016 upsets this assumption. Attempts have been made to explain it in terms of sport specifics of football *per se*. However, this conventional explanation will not stand up, for at least two reasons. First, the achievement of the men's football team was not an isolated phenomenon. As stated above, all the main Icelandic national teams have reached similar status in recent years. Second, these national teams in different sports have important characteristics in common. They are built on the same social-oriented principles and represent a certain cultural way of playing sport (see Chapters 6 and 7). This book is therefore not a detailed analysis of the teams in question but a sociological account of a specific national sports culture. In the following chapters I will show how this culture has helped this tiny nation to punch above its weight in different international sports. I propose to use sociological theory and empirical data in order to illustrate how culture works as a link between social structures and individual and group action, and how the general culture appears in how all the Icelandic teams play.

In the following chapters I will situate the achievements of the Icelandic national sport teams in the local cultural and historical context of Icelandic society. I will try to shift the focus from simplistic individual-level cause-and-effect explanations of Iceland's achievements to more dynamic socio-cultural explanations, experienced at the collective level. I have divided the content of this book into five sections.

In the first section (Chapters 1–3) I set the scene. The first chapter introduced the case of the Icelandic teams. In Chapter 2, I challenge the existing literature on sport success and achievement, outline the theoretical context of the case and describe the methods used in this study. Chapter 3 provides a short description of the history of sports in Iceland and describes the formal and social organization of sports in the country. In Section 2 (Chapters 4 and 5) I examine "how Iceland progressed" and focus on how the successful traditions of the teams in question were established in Iceland. Chapter 4 focuses on how Icelandic sports have in recent years moved towards professionalism. In Chapter 5 I further argue that these changes in the Icelandic sports culture benefitted a generation of athletes born in the 1980s and 1990s, which has helped the Icelandic teams reach new heights. In Section 3 (Chapters 6 and 7) I highlight how Icelanders play sport. The argument in Chapter 6 is that the Icelandic teams don't consist of world-class players but the Icelanders instead place great emphasis on showing good character in sports and to "play with their hearts." Chapter 7 further highlights the teamwork in the Icelandic teams, which is built around friendships, national pride and sacrifice for the greater good. Section 4 (Chapters 8 and 9) further shows how culture affects sports in Iceland. In Chapter 8 I argue that Icelandic sports have become more professional but not professional and represent an ideal relationship between an amateur approach *to* playing sport and profes-sional way *of* playing sport. Chapter 9 further identifies advantages of the small population of Iceland for the national teams. Finally, in Section 5 (Chapter 10) I propose a theory of how different cultural elements come together, at the same time, and provide Iceland with the important ingredients that all the aforemen-tioned teams are built upon.

Notes

1 "Ramon Calderón: Kalla þetta íslenska kraftaverkið" (news clip; *Visir.is.*, 2016, March). See: www.visir.is/section/MEDIA99&fileid=CLP43900
2 "Ekki jafn vinsælt frá Eyjafjallajökulgosi" (article; *Mbl.is.*, 2016, July). See: www.mbl.is/frettir/innlent/2016/06/28/island_ekki_jafn_vinsaelt_fra_eldgosinu_4/
3 "Afrek íslenska landsliðsins á forsíðum miðla út um allan heim" (article; *Kjarninn.is.*, 2015, September). See: http://kjarninn.is/frettir/afrek-islenska-landslidsins-a-forsidum-midla-ut-um-allan-heim/

12   *Setting the scene*

4 "Íslenska landsliðið í fimmta sæti" (article; *Mbl.is.*, 2013, February). See: www. mbl.is/sport/handbolti/2013/12/02/islenska_landslidid_i_fimmta_saeti/
5 The men's handball team won the B-World Cup Championship in 1988, which was at the time one of the high points in the history of Icelandic sports.
6 "Strákarnir upp í 22. sæti á FIFA listanum" (article; *Visir.is.*, 2016, June). See: www.ruv.is/frett/strakarnir-upp-i-22-saeti-a-fifa-listanum
7 "Ísland er stærsta litla fótboltalandið" (article; *Visir.is.*, 2016, June). See: www. visir.is/island-er-staersta-litla-fotboltalandid/article/2016160719813
8 Eygló Ósk Gústafsdóttir, a female swimmer, was chosen for the Sportsperson of the Year award in 2015.
9 "Óskar Bjarni í Akraborginni: Stærðfræði, íslenska og handbolti" (article; *Sport. is.*, 2015, October). See: http://sport.moi.is/handbolti/2015/10/28/oskar-bjarni-i-akraborginni-staerdfraedi-islenska-og-handbolti/

References

Beamish, R. and Ritchie, I. (2006). *Fastest, highest, strongest: A critique of high-performance sport*. London: Routledge.
Becker, H.S. (2007). *Telling about society*. Chicago: The University of Chicago Press.
Bloomfield, J. (2003). *Australia's sporting success: The inside story*. Kensington: University of New South Wales Press.
Cashmore, E. (2002). *Sport psychology: The key concepts*. London: Routledge.
Epstein, D. (2013). *The sports gene: Inside the science of extraordinary athletic performance*. New York: Penguin.
Hill, M. (2007). *In pursuit of excellence*. London: Routledge.
Kuper, S. and Szimansky, S. (2014). *Soccernomics*. London: HarperSport.
Sam, M. (2016). Youth sport policy in small nations. In K. Green and A. Smith (eds.), *Routledge handbook of youth sport* (pp. 535–542). London: Routledge.
Steinarsson, S.Ó. (1994). *Strákarnir okkar: Saga landsliðsins í handknattleik 1950–1993*. Reykjavík: Fróði.
Thorlindsson, T. and Halldorsson, V. (2017). The cultural production of a successful sport tradition: A case study of Icelandic handball. *Studies in Symbolic Interaction* (in press).
Wieting, S. (2015). *The sociology of hypocrisy: An analysis of sport and religion*. London: Routledge.

2 From nature and nurture, to culture

Theoretical basis and methods

No man is his own creation.

– Grettir Ásmundarson (Grettissaga, 1946, 41)

Nature or nurture?

Much of the academic literature dealing with the sources of individual differences, in regard to expert performance, has emphasized particularistic talent (see, for instance, Abbott et al., 2005). This emphasis is particularly evident in regard to excellence in sports. The theories on talent have rested on two main pillars; that talent is either inborn (nature) or that it can be acquired (nurture). Numerous studies have been carried out in the literature to date, representing either side.

The literature has overwhelmingly emphasized the nature side of talent in regard to sporting achievement (Entine, 2001; Klissouras, Geladas and Koskolou, 2007; Lock and Palsson, 2016). Nature proponents presume that inborn talent specifies a correlation with intrinsic genes/hormones and key physical demands associated with any sporting behavior (see Posthumus and Collins, 2016). Such views are deterministic and reductionist, limiting access to sporting success to those who possess the right genes that fit with the specified physical performance.

The nature favorers' ideas have been used to describe collective success, experienced on a national level. Conspicuous sports success among people of particular races or local origins is likewise commonly attributed to genetics, with the notion that athletes from specific origins are better equipped than others for certain sports in terms of their genes. The world-class successes of Kenyan and Ethiopian middle- and long-distance runners (MacArthur and North, 2007), and of sprinters from Jamaica, are clear examples of this type (see Epstein, 2014).

Interestingly, such hereditary explanations have mainly been applied to the emerging cases of world-class black athletes in certain sports (Entine,

2001; Hoberman, 1998). Coakley, for instance, has argued that this line of explanation – attributing sporting success to genes – has been used to create racial classification systems, with particular types of achievement being associated with black athletes (Coakley and Pike, 2009).

It is tempting to utilize genetic explanations for the achievements of Icelandic teams. Icelandic athletes are frequently compared to the Vikings from the Icelandic sagas. They are seen as brave and heroic ambassadors of the nation who fight tough battles against much larger and stronger nations – their strong and powerful oppressors. It is in this light that Icelanders tend to liken their brave athletes to the Vikings, with the indication that they come from Viking stock; this is analogous, in a strange way, to what was claimed concerning Icelandic bankers and investors in the 2000s (Durrenberger and Palsson, 2015).

Iceland's economic boom in the 2000s was based on the international activities of Icelandic bankers and investors who made massive investments in businesses worldwide (see Bjorgolfsson, 2014). They came from tiny Iceland to conquer major marketplaces and their success inspired the designation "Outvasion Vikings." This name was linked with increased prosperity in Iceland, which resulted in higher living standards and a sense of overconfidence on the part of the Icelandic nation (Durrenberger and Palsson, 2015). The general narrative of those successful bankers was linked to the gene pool of the Icelandic Vikings, showing them as strong and fearless against any odds. This emphasis on genetics contributed to self-confidence, positive self-identity and national pride for the Icelandic people, who on such occasions are prone to cite their origin from the same gene pool as the great Vikings.

Scholars have, however, been skeptical of stereotypes based on the outstanding "gene pool" of the Icelanders. When the Icelandic banks crashed in 2008 and some of the most conspicuous Outvasion Vikings were sent to prison, Icelanders realized that their "success" had nothing to do with the genetic superiority of the Icelandic stock. Most Icelanders now deny having participated in or supported this narrative (see Durrenberger and Palsson, 2015). They tend to hold on to such accounts when they do well as a nation, but are quick to abandon them when they fail. According to anthropologist Loftsdottir (2015, 4) the emergence of the economic crisis "created a paradigm shift in which this narrative [of the successful genetically superior Business Viking] lost its power almost overnight." The aftermath of the financial crash further led to mass protests and riots in Iceland (Bernburg, 2016). Interestingly, genetics were used to explain the financial "successes" of Icelandic bankers but not to explain their failures and excesses, which contributed to the financial meltdown in Iceland in 2008 (Pálsson and Guðbjörnsson, 2011, 138).

Just as the attribution of achievement to genes proved to be, at best, inconsistent, the investigation of the part played by genes in expert performance has proved unsupported, problematic and unsatisfactory. While some evidence exists on the relationship between genetic heredity and physical attributes (Klissouras, Geladas and Koskolou, 2007) researchers have not been able to identify specific sporting genes (Bale and Sang, 1996; Bures, 2016; Davids and Baker, 2007; Scott et al., 2007). Farrey argues that it would require the examination of "at least 124 genes and thousands, perhaps millions, of combinations of those genes, and this would provide only part of an explanation" (Coakley and Pike, 2009, 322). Further studies on genetics of individuals and groups have proved inadequate for understanding elite performance. Accordingly, researchers have increasingly turned their attention to the influence of the social environment (Davids and Baker, 2007; Henrich, 2016).

During the mid-twentieth century, nurture theories began to evolve and have gained empirical support (Bailey and Morley, 2006; Baker et al., 2003; Hay and MacDonald, 2010; Henrich, 2016). Nurturist theories reject the deterministic and reductionist explanations proposed by adherents of the nature-based explanations and argue instead that high achievers have, through their immediate environment, been nurtured to succeed in their field, and particularly through practice and individual socialization.

Nurturists have especially emphasized the importance of practice to gain excellence. Ericsson (1996) has noted that expert performance, in a wide range of activities, such as elite sports, rests on at least 10,000 hours of "deliberate practice" in the field. The assumption behind this idea is that it is not "what you are made of" that matters, it is "what you do." Research on the nurture part of sport achievement has furthermore emphasized the importance of socialization as a key social influence favoring the emergence of talented athletes (see Ericsson et al., 2006). This research places special focus on the family unit, and also on coaches and teachers, as important socializing agents (Bloom, 1985; Carlson, 1988; Kay, 2000; Woolger and Power, 1993). These parties are seen as "nurturing" individuals towards doing certain activities in certain ways, committing themselves to deliberate practice, resembling ritual.

While many scholars have argued that the nature-versus-nurture debate is outdated – and have proposed an increased multidisciplinary and integrative scientific focus on the roots of expert performance – they nevertheless recognize an important interaction between nature and nurture. While innate talent can give individuals an advantage, without nurturing that talent, they are not likely to reach the elite level (Epstein, 2014; Philips et al., 2010; Starkes and Ericsson, 2003).

But even when the nature and nurture viewpoints are both recognized this theoretical basis still lacks specificity (Lock and Palsson, 2016).[1] This research fails to account for the involvement of the social actor in social networks and relationships (Granovetter, 1986; Henrich, 2016). Fine (2015) argues that "Nature and nurture depend on a network, a basis of social relations that permit genetics and socialization to have consequences" (23). Even playing an individualistic game (relatively speaking) such as chess (stressing individual expertise) involves a collective domain shaped by collective standards, which exists outside the two competing chess players (Fine, 2015). Even though the nurturists provided a necessary corrective of genetics, the over-emphasis on practice and socialization has, for instance, drawn attention away from the wider social context of sporting achievement. Of course, socialization is of central importance in mediating social influences and shaping individual behavior. However, other aspects of social organization contained within the social organization of groups also need to be considered (Thorlindsson, 2011). These social mechanisms exist at the group level and their influences cannot be reduced to the individual level. Thus, the wider socio-cultural context has been overlooked in research on excellence and achievement (Davids and Baker, 2007; Epstein, 2014; Lock and Palsson, 2016). Human evolutionary biologist Joseph Henrich has argued this case, emphasizing that the rise of the human species to dominate the globe is not the result of our innate intelligence, but of our "collective brains":

> The secret of our species' success resides not in the power of our individual minds, but in the *collective brains* of our communities. Our collective brains arise from the synthesis of our cultural and social natures – from the fact that we readily learn from others (are cultural) and can, with the right norms, live in large and widely interconnected groups (are social).
>
> (2016, 5)

Thus, in this book I will "take the road less traveled" and analyze the achievements of the Icelandic national teams on a collective level by studying the local social, cultural and historical context that influences and shapes Icelandic sports in general.

The local social, cultural and historical context

Numerous examples from the current sports scene strongly suggest that attention needs to be paid to the socio-cultural context of sports performance. Physiology and individual psychology alone do not easily explain the success of Brazilian and Argentinian soccer; Canadian ice hockey; Croatian, Swedish and Icelandic handball; or even Kenyan and Ethiopian middle- and long-distance running. Such cases call for an understanding of the cultural and social context of the different places and societies, which are captured by neither an emphasis on nature nor on nurture. While an abundance of research on the interdependence of sport and society in the sociology of sports exists, research on the cultural and collective basis of sports performance is limited. Even analysis of effective teamwork in sport as well as in other domains generally ignores the role of culture (see West, 2012). All athletes need a tradition, which consists of values, motivation, social support and knowledge, and a window of opportunity. A successful athlete needs a community that prepares him for the world of sports. Much of that preparation can be found in the social and cultural environment that is taken for granted and embedded in the mundane activities of daily life.[2]

The sociological approach, used in this book, is to treat a national sport success as a cultural production, in which the actions of individual and groups are "the consequence *and* cause of society" (Fine, 2012, 54), instead of focusing on specific sports or individual heroes – as is customary in the general discourse.

Such meso-level analysis rests on two main notions. The first notion states that culture and social structures shape and restrict the behavior of individuals and groups through traditions, societal norms and values, as well as affect individual's self-identity, action and the meanings people associate with certain behavior in society (Mead, [1934]/1972). This view is echoed in those of Goffman ([1959]/1990), who claimed that individual public performances come to reflect the official values of society and serve as a reaffirmation of the moral values of the whole community. Thus, different cultures emphasize different activities and provide different meanings that produce different results.

However, Fine argues that:

> Sociologists have often ignored the idea that culture is a form of performance within a local context, with meaning derived from those contextual features, while treating culture as a thing in itself, separate from how it is used in practice.
>
> (2012, 34)

This leads to the second notion, which states that culture is also a system of shared meanings that derive from interaction. Culture should therefore not only be understood as an independent variable – directly affecting individuals and groups – but also as a dependent variable that is influenced by social interaction (Blumer, 1969). Interaction forms the basis of culture where the interaction that people have with each other on a daily basis forms the foundations of social structures (Goffman, 1967). Therefore, as Fine states, all groups build their own "ideoculture," which consists of "a system of knowledge, beliefs, behaviors, and customs shared by members of an interacting group to which members refer and that they employ as the basis of further interaction" (2012, 36).

In his study of Little League baseball, Fine (1987) argues that while each team had its own ideoculture, the teams were based on a similar structure. Hence, the theoretical stand proposed in this book states that all groups within a specific culture or tradition are, in this light, unique but also the same.

Several scholars have analyzed the development of national sports and the local variations in the playing style of sports teams in such terms. There are fine examples of such studies have been important in this respect: of Argentinian football (Archetti, 1999), Australian athletes (Bloomfield, 2003), Brazilian football (Lever, [1983]/1995), curling in Canada (Wieting and Lamoureux, 2001); East African middle- and long-distance runners (Bale and Sang, 1996; Pitsiladis et al., 2007), Finnish hockey players (Lamsa, 2012), and sprinters from Jamaica (Moore, 2015). These scholars have suggested that traditional culture forms the basis for the great traditions of national achievements in sport.

This book will build on sociological analysis, more precisely on what Fine (2012) has termed as "a sociology of the local" (157–177) centering on the small Icelandic community. The approach focuses on how local worlds in such context imbue action with meaning, which strengthens common values and incorporates cultural continuity (Fine, 2012, 163). Thus, the key argument of this book is that the national team sport success of Iceland is culturally produced and in order to understand such collective achievement in more depth, we need to shift the focus from nature and nurture, to culture, and turn our attention to the local socio-cultural and historical context of Iceland. This book provides support for this claim by analyzing Iceland's sporting success, framing it theoretically and then investigating it empirically.

Methods

In the process of viewing, specifically, Icelandic sports, I am largely influenced by the principal theoretical ideas of Howard S. Becker (1998; 2007; [1982]/2008; 2014), who argued that sociology should study collective action, that collective action occurs in steps and that comparison is central to sociological analysis (Becker, [1982]/2008, xi–xii). Becker stated:

> Research that looks at objects differs from research that looks at processes in several important ways. First of all, if you look at objects alone, you don't see how they got to be the kind of objects they are.

Since you don't see it you imagine it. But of course, for scientists it is always better to see something happen than to imagine how it happened.

(Lu, 2015, 137)

Cases link ideas and evidence. Case studies provide theoretical and analytical tools to examine such socio-historical and cultural phenomena as the Icelandic sport case. In order to understand the processes of social action the researcher has to go back and forth between data and theory. The dynamic interplay between the empirical and theoretical is crucial in this context. Ragin (1992) further notes that "Casing is an essential part of the process of producing theoretical structured descriptions of social life and of using empirical evidence to articulate theories" (225). This is my goal.

While this study builds on the principal theoretical ideas of Becker, a case study design, as proposed by Yin (2014), was used to validate the findings. The empirical investigation is based on "thick data" (see Ragin and Amoroso, 2011). More specifically, it is based on the following seven actions and sources. First, I conducted 39 formal interviews with various people associated with Icelandic sports and the teams in question (see the Appendix). These include former and current coaches (including coaches of all the teams that first made their mark since 2008), former and current players, staff members, sports administrators, sports historians, sports broadcasters and sports fans. The interviews were focused on the teams in question and also broader sporting issues in Iceland. I also interviewed foreign sports administrators, coaches and players in order to establish a comparison to the Icelandic case and obtain outside views on the structure of Icelandic sport and Icelandic players. The interviews were conducted in four countries (Iceland, Denmark, Germany and the Netherlands) and via Skype. The ages of the interviewees ranged from 27 to 76, 31 men and 8 women, 31 Icelanders and 8 foreigners. The interviews were semistructured and lasted from 40 minutes up to two hours. They sometimes took the form of discussions – or mutual exploration – with my interviewees, of the themes in question. They were all (but two) transcribed and coded into themes.

Second, I had dozens of informal talks and discussions with various people associated with sport in Iceland: members of the general public and foreign press journalists who came to Iceland to cover the successes of the Icelandic national teams. These talks were mainly used to obtain a feeling for the *zeitgeist*, gain fresh insights into the subject, make comparisons with other cultures and validate the emerging themes. I took notes at these discussions, but did not use the material for direct quotations in this book.

Third, one of my arguments is that the achievements of the Icelandic national teams cannot be understood by looking only at sports in Iceland

and that they have to be understood through an analysis of the general Icelandic culture as well. I had informal discussions about Icelandic culture with my colleagues in the departments of Sociology, Anthropology, History and Psychology as well as with other individuals with knowledge or thoughts on the subject.

Fourth, the case study also consists of ethnographic observations. I have been present at the games of the Icelandic teams in the big tournaments (such as the 2016 European Championship in men's football in France). I also visited four European professional football clubs for the research for this book, where I watched training, conducted formal interviews, had informal talks with coaches and explored the club's facilities.

Fifth, I build on my own experience. For the past fifteen years I have been a prominent sports consultant in Iceland. I have worked for some of the teams, with some of the members of those teams and been present at training and games and team meetings. My consulting work has provided me with unique access and perspective for analyzing the topic in question. In the past four years I have also collected field notes on the Icelandic sport scene specifically.

Sixth, living in Iceland situates me in the midst of the action. I have been involved in the Icelandic sports scene for around forty years, first in playing sports as a child, then playing many sports in my teenage years and handball at the senior level, coaching all ages in sports such as football and handball and doing consulting work in Icelandic sports. I am closely linked to the sports network in Iceland where the smallness of Icelandic society unavoidably connects me to people involved in the action. My brother is a former women's national handball coach; my nephew is a member of the men's football team and I personally know most of the members as well as most of the coaches of those teams. In this book I base my analysis partly on these experiences.[3]

Seventh, the case study draws on published material, such as books, articles, documentaries and various other data sources, such as coaches' seminars (with the men's football and handball teams), media coverage, internet blogs, and social network discussions.

The findings are based on empirical data. The interviews provided strong confirmation of the main underlying themes that emerged in this study of how Iceland managed to do well in sport at the international level. Thus, the findings highlighted what Becker termed "representations of society"; that is, something that someone told me about some aspect of social life that I did not necessarily experience first-hand (Becker, 2007, 5). These descriptions and narratives illuminated the commonplace social mechanisms that contributed to the collective success of the Icelandic national sports teams (Faulkner and Becker, 2009, 196–197). The findings are presented in a theory-building structure (see Yin, 2014) where each chapter reveals a new addition to the theoretical argument. I validated the themes that emerged from the case analysis by using multiple data sources as well as by obtaining confirmation of the main findings from selected participants. The data were analyzed using MAXQDA12 software.

Notes

1 The general view of the prerequisites of excellence and achievement crystalizes in a recent article by a columnist, Adam Kilgore, in the Washington Post entitled "U.S. athletes run fast, jump high, throw hard – why are we so bad in handball?" The article highlights physical attributes and practice as the fundamental elements for sporting success, ignoring the role of culture (article; *Washingtonpost.com.*, 2016, August). See: www.washingtonpost.com/sports/olympics/us-athletes-run-fast-jump-high-throw-hard – why-are-we-so-bad-at-handball/2016/08/09/39236262–5e25–11e6-af8e-54aa2e849447_story.html?utm_term=.de23cec32c4a
2 Parts of this text were co-written by Þórólfur Þórlindsson.
3 A good text on the challenges of objectivity, which I had in mind in the research process, is Norbert Elias's Involvement and Detachment ([1956]/1987).

References

Abbott, A., Button, C., Pepping, G-J. and Collins, D. (2005). Unnatural selection: Talent identification and development in sport. *Nonlinear Dynamics, Psychology, and Life Sciences*, 9(1): 61–88.
Archetti, E.P. (1999). *Masculinities: Football, polo and the tango in Argentina.* Oxford: Berg.
Bailey, R. and Morley, D. (2006). Towards a model of talent development in physical education. *Sport, Education and Society*, 11: 211–230.
Baker, J., Horton, S., Robertson-Wilson, J. and Wall, M. (2003). Nurturing sport expertise: Factors influencing the development of elite athletes. *Journal of Sport Sciences and Medicine*, 2: 1–9.
Bale, J. and Sang, J. (1996). *Kenyan running: Movement, culture, geography and global change.* London: Frank Cass.
Becker, H.S. ([1982]/2008). *Art worlds.* Berkeley: University of California Press.
Becker, H.S. (1998). *Tricks of the trade. How to think about research while you're doing it.* Chicago: The University of Chicago Press.
Becker, H.S. (2007). *Telling about society.* Chicago: The University of Chicago Press.
Becker, H.S. (2014). *What about Mozart? What about murder? Reasoning from cases.* Chicago: The University of Chicago Press.
Bernburg, J.G. (2016). *Economic crisis and mass protest: The pots and pans revolution in Iceland.* London: Routlege.

Bjorgolfsson, T. (2014). *Billions to bust and back: How I made, lost and rebuilt a fortune, and what I learned along the way.* London: Profile Books.

Bloom, B. (1985). *Developing talent in young people.* New York: Ballantine.

Bloomfield, J. (2003). *Australia's sporting success: The inside story.* Kensington: University of New South Wales Press.

Blumer, H. (1969). *Symbolic interactionism: Perspective and method.* Englewood Cliffs, NJ: Prentice-Hall.

Bures, F. (2016). Running circles around us: East African Olympians' advantage may be more than physical. *Scientific American.* Available online at: www.scientificamerican.com/article/running-circles-around-us . . . -african-olympians-advantage-may-be-more-than-physical/?print=true

Carlson, R. (1988). The socialization of elite tennis players in Sweden: An analysis of the players' backgrounds and development. *Sociology of Sport Journal,* 5: 241–256.

Coakley, J. and Pike, E. (2009). *Sports in society: Issues and controversies.* London: McGraw-Hill.

Davids, K. and Baker, J. (2007). Genes, environment and sport performance. Why the nature-nurture dualism is no longer relevant. *Sports Medicine,* 37(11): 961–980.

Durrenberger, E.P., and Palsson, G. (eds.) (2015). *Gambling debt: Iceland's rise and fall in the global economy.* Boulder: University Press of Colorado.

Elias, N. ([1956]/1987). Involvement and detachment. *British Journal of Sociology,* 7(3): 226–252.

Entine, J. (2001). *Taboo: Why black athletes dominate sports and why we're afraid to talk about it.* New York: Public Affairs.

Epstein, D. (2014). *The sports gene: Inside the science of extraordinary athletic performance.* New York: Penguin.

Ericsson, K.A. (ed.) (1996). *The road to excellence: The acquisition of expert performance in the arts and sciences, sports, and games.* Mahwah, NJ: Erlbaum.

Ericsson, K.A., Charness, N., Feltovich, P.J. and Hoffman, R.R. (eds.) (2006). *The Cambridge handbook of expertise and expert performance.* Cambridge: Cambridge University Press.

Faulkner, R.R. and Becker, H.S. (2009). *"Do you know. . . ?" The jazz repertoire in action.* Chicago: The University of Chicago Press.

Fine, G.A. (1987). *With the boys: Little league baseball and preadolescent culture.* Chicago: The University of Chicago University Press.

Fine, G.H. (2012). *Tiny publics: A theory of group action and culture.* New York: Russell Sage Foundation.

Fine, G.H. (2015). *Players and pawns: How chess builds community and culture.* Chicago: The University of Chicago University Press.

Goffman, E. ([1959]/1990). *The presentation of self in everyday life.* London: Penguin Books.

Goffman, E. (1967). *Interaction ritual: Essays on face-to-face behavior.* New York: Anchor Books.

From nature and nurture, to culture   23

Granovetter, M. (1986). Economic action and social structure: The problem of embeddedness. *American Journal of Sociology*, 91: 481–510.

Grettissaga (1946). Reykjavík: Helgafell.

Hay, W.F. and MacDonald, D. (2010). Evidence for the social construction of ability in physical education. *Sport, Education and Society*, 15: 1–18.

Henrich, J. (2016). *The secret of our success*. Princeton: Princeton University Press.

Hoberman, J. (1998). *Darwin's athletes: How sport has damaged black America and preserved the myth of the race*. Boston: Mariner Books.

Kay, T. (2000). Sporting excellence: A family affair? *European Physical Education Review*, 6: 151–169.

Klissouras, V., Geladas, N. and Koskolou, M. (2007). Nature prevails over nurture. *International Journal of Sport Psychology*, 38: 35–67.

Lamsa, J. (2012). Lions on the ice: The success story of Finnish ice hockey. In S.S. Andersen and L.T. Ronglan (eds.), *Nordic elite sport: Same ambitions, different tracks* (pp. 83–106). Oslo: Universitetsforlaget.

Lever, J. ([1983]/1995). *Soccer madness: Brazil's passion for the world's most popular sport*. Chicago, IL: Waveland Press.

Lock, M. and Palsson, G. (2016): *Can science resolve the nature/nurture debate?* Cambridge: Polity.

Loftsdottir, K. (2015). Vikings invade present-day Iceland. In E.P. Durrenberger and G. Palsson (eds.) *Gambling debt: Iceland's rise and fall in the global economy* (pp. 3–14). Boulder: University Press of Colorado.

Lu, W. (2015). Sociology and art: An interview with Howard S. Becker. *Symbolic Interaction*, 38 (1): 127–150.

MacArthur, D.G. and North, K.N. (2007). Genes and human elite athletic performance. In Y. Pitsiladis, J. Bale, C. Sharp and T. Noakes (eds.), *East-African running: Towards a cross-disciplinary perspective* (pp. 217–233). London: Routledge.

Mead, G.H. ([1934]/1972). *Mind, self & society: From a standpoint of a social behaviorist*. Chicago: The University of Chicago press.

Moore, R. (2015). *The Bolt supremacy: Inside Jamaica's sprint factory*. London: Yellow Jersey Press.

Pálsson, G. and Guðbjörnsson, S.Ö. (2011). Make no bones about it: The invention of Homo Islandicus. *Acta Borealia*, 28(2): 119–141.

Philips, A., Davids, K., Renshaw, I. and Portus, M. (2010). Expert performance in sport and the dynamics of talent development. *Sports Medicine*, 40: 271–283.

Pitsiladis, Y., Bale, J., Sharp, C. and Noakes, T. (eds.) (2007). *East-African running: Towards a cross-disciplinary perspective*. London: Routledge.

Posthumus, M. and Collins, M. (2016). *Genetics and sport*. Basel: Karger.

Ragin C.C. (1992). Casing and the process of social inquiry. In C.C. Ragin and H.S. Becker (eds.), *What is a case? Exploring the foundations of social inquiry* (pp. 217–226). Cambridge: Cambridge University Press.

Ragin, C.C. and Amoroso, L.M. (2011). *Constructing social research*. Los Angeles: Sage.

Scott, R.A., Goodwin, W.H., Wolde, B., Onywera, V.O., Boit, M.K., O'Connell, W. and Pitsiladis, Y. (2007). Evidence for the 'natural' East African athlete. In Y. Pitsiladis, J. Bale, C. Sharp and T. Noakes (eds.), *East-African running: Towards a cross-disciplinary perspective* (pp. 257–282). London: Routledge.

Starkes, J. and Ericsson, K.A. (2003). *Expert performance in sports: Advances in research and sport expertise*. Champaign, IL: Human Kinetics.

Thorlindsson, T. (2011). Bring in the social context: Towards an integrated approach to health promotion and prevention. *Scandinavian Journal of Public Health*, 39(6): 19–25.

West, M.A. (2012). *Effective teamwork: Practical lessons from organizational research*. London: Wiley-Blackwell.

Wieting, S.G. and Lamoureux, D. (2001). Curling in Canada. *Culture, Sport, Society*, 4(2): 140–154.

Woolger, C. and Power, T.G. (1993). Parent and sport socialization: Views from the achievement literature. *Journal of Sport Behavior*, 16: 171–190.

Yin, R.K. (2014). *Case study research: Design and methods*. Los Angeles: Sage.

3   The social and structural organization of sport in Iceland

Studies of sport which are not studies of society are studies out of context.
                                                    – Norbert Elias (Elias and Dunning, 1986, 26).

Iceland

Iceland is a 103,000-km^2 volcanic island in the middle of the North Atlantic. With a population of 330,000, it is the most sparsely populated country in Europe. It is one of the Nordic nations – along with Denmark, Finland, Norway and Sweden.

In the Age of Settlement (870–930) people from Norway and Celtic-populated areas under Norse domination began to settle in Iceland. After four centuries of autonomy Iceland came under Norwegian crown, later being absorbed with Norway into the Danish kingdom. The nineteenth century saw the rise of nationalistic sentiments among the Icelandic people and the campaign for independence from the Danish rule became important (Jónsson, 1983). Iceland received its independence in 1918 and became a republic in 1944.

The Nordic nations are built on similar foundations, characterized by an emphasis on Protestantism, social democracy and the welfare state (Meinander, 1998). But according to Karlsson (1995) during the time of Nordic occupancy, the people of Iceland maintained a separate identity from their occupants, an identity that was formed by the Icelandic sagas and the Icelandic language. Recently, Mixa and Vaiman (2015) argued that despite Iceland's social democratic roots and its connection to the Scandinavian nations, individualism is much more valued among the Icelandic people than among their neighbors in Scandinavia. Thus, although Iceland has a lot in common with the other Nordic nations it has – due partly to its geographical isolation – developed its own specific culture, language and characteristics

(Wieting, 2015). The Icelandic novelist Jón Kalmann Stefánsson's description of Iceland is appropriate in this context:

> Icelandic history is a history of isolation. A large island in a northern sea, with a magnificent yet unforgiving natural environment and a trying climate. Icelandic society was inert, experiencing little or no change for centuries. Villages and towns did not exist until the late 19th century; there was little class division and the life of the inhabitants was work, work and more work.[1]

Iceland went from being among the poorest nations in Europe in the mid-nineteenth century to one of the wealthiest and most developed nations in the world in the late twentieth century. Modern Iceland is an affluent society characterized by a market economy and a strong social welfare system. The affluence of Icelandic society is largely due to the rich fishing grounds around the country. Fishing has been the leading industry of Iceland, which has generally been described as "a fishing nation." Around two-thirds of the population lives in the capital, Reykjavik, and the surrounding areas in the southwest corner of the country. The rest of the population mostly lives in small towns and villages on the coast around the country.

The weather plays a big part in the daily lives of Icelanders. It is typified by long, cold and dark winters and short and bright summers. Iceland has been ethnically and religiously a homogenous nation and often referred to as a "classless" society, meaning that class divisions are not as profound as in many other nations – such as in Britain and the United States. Iceland is furthermore the only NATO member that does not maintain a standing army.

Historical notes on the organization of sport in Iceland

The sporting history of Iceland reaches back to its early settlers, and sports have been practiced, in one way or the other, throughout the nation's history. In the first centuries after the settlement, sports were a popular activity frequently referred to in the famous Icelandic sagas (see Bjarnason, 1908; Finnbogason, [1933]/1971, 128; Wieting, 2015). More specifically, in 24 sagas there are 88 references to sport and games (see Wieting, 2015, 72–77). The sagas were important for the building of the Icelandic national identity (Loftsdottir, 2015), in which the saga writers saw men of the Viking age as strongmen, competing in games with weapons, wrestling, swimming and, particularly, in various ball games (Jónsson, 1983). These games were characterized by the concept of honor and rules of fairness (Wieting, 2015, 78). Sports were a social activity and such games were sometimes played at social festivals with attending spectators (Jónsson, 1906, 357).

The practice of sport and games varied in popularity through the ages; obviously, deteriorating climate, natural catastrophes and material privation led to reduced prominence of sports in some periods. In his analysis of Icelandic culture in the years leading to modernity, Finnbogason ([1933]/1971, 129) has noted that "Few people are gifted with the noble ambition of competing with themselves." Sports in Iceland were based on social action, which involved competition, so in harsh times when social gatherings became less frequent, the participation rate in games of sports was reduced. Sports, however, survived through the ages and have been a significant activity in the history of the Icelandic nation.

The dramatic changes that followed industrialization and urbanization of Icelandic society – as in European nations in the eighteenth century – provided a platform and opportunities for the development of modern sports. Increased communication with other nations introduced Icelanders to new sports which the Icelandic people adapted and started playing (Jónsson, 1983). The last two decades of the nineteenth century marked the foundations of modern sports in Iceland. Sports clubs were established in which Danish influences were particularly strong; Iceland was under the Danish rule and many of the pioneers who established the sporting scene in Iceland had lived and studied in Denmark. When they came back home to Iceland they brought with them the sports they learned in their host country.

The twentieth century saw the rise of modern sports in Iceland. This was evident in the growth of sports clubs, which were established in many districts and towns and intended to serve the local community. Sports were introduced in schools and taken up in the school curriculum. The Icelandic Youth Association (UMFÍ) was established in 1906 and six years later saw the establishment of the National Olympic and Sports Association (ÍSÍ), which is still the main authority of formal sport in Iceland.

The establishment of the sport clubs and associations at the turn of the twentieth century marked the first high point of modern sport in Iceland. According to Valgeirsson (1991), the first sports clubs were in part built around nationalistic sentiments and were important in Iceland's campaign for independence from Denmark. Sports became a vehicle for nationalism. Hobsbawm has argued that sport in the Nordic countries "became an important tool in the mass production of invented traditions" because of the absence of military ambitions and great power politics in the Nordic countries (in Meinander, 1998, 5). This argument is especially relevant in Iceland. The Icelandic Youth Association (UMFÍ) was established around the movement for independence from Denmark at the turn of the twentieth century. Auður Inga Þorsteinsdóttir, secretary-general of the Icelandic Youth Association, reflects on the first years of the association:

It started up during the independence campaign. That's exactly what it was about: to stand firm and get through it. It was completely intertwined with the history of the UMFÍ. And the youth clubs at the time, in all parts of the country, they were the driving force for doing something in society. Nowadays it's very much concentrated around sports, but in those days it wasn't.

The campaign for independence furthermore created room for nationalistic sentiments that was in part filled by the nation's obsession with sports. At the Olympic Games in Stockholm in 1912, the Icelandic contestants in Icelandic *glíma* – which was an exhibition sport at the Games – protested against Danish rule in Iceland: they wanted to take part in the opening ceremony of the Games under the Icelandic flag, and not under the Danish. Denmark objected to this act of provocation by the Icelandic athletes, who in turn boycotted the opening ceremony of the Games (Jørgensen, 1998).

The introduction and establishment of formal sports in Iceland was the work of only a handful of enthusiastic men.[2] When they departed from the scene, the national emphasis on sport dwindled. On the one hand, the drive of the originators could not be maintained. On the other hand, interest waned because of the impact of the two world wars on daily life in Iceland. Sports were not to be a prominent feature in Icelandic society again until after World War II. The year 1946 stands out as the beginning of a new era in Icelandic sports. It was the first time in the history of this tiny nation that it made its mark in international sporting competition, and a decade of great sporting achievements followed, mostly in track and field; this period of time became known as *frjálsíþróttavorið* ("the spring of Icelandic athletics"). The high point of this great decade of Icelandic sport success occurred when Vilhjálmur Einarsson won a silver medal in the triple jump competition at the 1956 Olympics in Melbourne. Two years later the men's handball team qualified for its first major championship. Interestingly, those historical achievements also ended the overtly successful period of Icelandic sports – in other sports than handball, which became the national sport of Iceland in the decades that followed. Sports historian Steinar J. Lúðvíksson argues that this ending was in part due to a political and cultural transformation of Icelandic society. At that time the nation was experiencing increased prosperity – after the war – which saw changes in governmental policy and the general lifestyle of Icelanders. Increased individualism and an emphasis on the pursuit of material goods shifted the focus of the nation to other areas. Iceland was becoming an affluent society and interest in sports *per se* became second to the pursuit of wealth.

Historians such as Lúðvíksson have argued that in the second half of the twentieth century, Iceland went from a sporting to an economic nation. Former national player in football, basketball and volleyball, and PE teacher and advocate, Anton Bjarnason strikes the same note. He remembers from his youth that sports were frowned upon and considered a waste of time. "Young people should dedicate their time to work, instead of playing around," was the mantra in the 1960s.

The decades around the millennium saw the next high point of sports in Iceland. This was founded on an international trend in sports, which scholars have termed "the sportization of society" (Crum, 1991). This comprises the belief that sports are seen as contributing an important function for the positive development of their participants. It led to a massive increase in participation in sports by all groups in society. This was also the case in Iceland. Increased participation at the level of sports clubs created a fertile ground for a new sport culture and further achievements by Icelandic athletes. Community-based sports clubs were increasingly seen as a convenient place to store children while both parents worked outside the home in the newly emerged capitalist society. The sports clubs were also seen as an important tool for the socialization of children and adolescents into society. This focus on socialization placed added responsibility on the clubs: not only did they stand for sports, but they also became social centers serving the local communities – especially children and adolescents. In turn, the clubs started paying salaries to all their coaches and coaches' qualifications became increasingly important.

Research on the effects of sport participation for children and adolescents, starting in the early 1990s, by Professor Þórólfur Þórlindsson and his colleagues, among other things, helped give rise to the general positive outlook of organized sports in Iceland. They showed that participation in sports – especially organized sports – has positive developmental outcomes for children and adolescents (Þórlindsson, Karlsson and Sigfúsdóttir, 1992; Þórlindsson et al., 1997; Þórlindsson et al., 2000). This sports trend took root in Iceland and pushed Icelandic sports further in the direction of community-level sports intended for everybody, in contrast to professional sports intended for the few, which became the dominant trend in many Western European countries. Sports became settled in the school curriculum intended for all children over the nine years of compulsory school. The schools also became linked to the organized sports clubs where it is custom that children go to practice at the local sports club straight after school. Due to the common belief that participation in organized sports is beneficial for children and adolescents, the municipalities subsidize club participation fees for children and adolescents. Some clubs and municipalities even provide bus trips for children between the schools and the clubs.

Sports clubs have established themselves as socially important for the promotion of health and fitness and for the general socialization of children and
adolescents.

Today, the sports clubs in Iceland are built on this model, which some
scholars have referred to as the "Nordic sports model"[3] (see Bairner, 2010).
The clubs receive funds from the state and municipalities but they retain
their autonomy in exchange for attending to the promotion of public health,
especially with an emphasis on sports for children and adolescents. They
serve as social centers that are open to all, and everyone has the chance to be
coached by appropriately educated and professional coaches from an early
age (which is not the case in many countries, such as in Scandinavia, where
parents are responsible for coaching kids' sports). The clubs are also under
the umbrella of the large, national and voluntary sports organizations, the
National Olympic and Sports Association (ÍSÍ), which has a near-monopoly
on competitive sports.

The scope of sport in Iceland

An Icelandic minister of Eduction, Science and Culture (and sport) has
described Icelanders as a "nation mad about sports."[4] Sports have become a
popular pastime in Iceland, as participation rates show, with around 90% of
all children taking part in organized sport at some point in time (Halldorsson, 2014). The peak of organized sport participation is among 10 year-olds:
over 80% of 6th graders practice sport in sport clubs (Halldorsson, 2014).
Participation rates tend to decline in the older year-classes, as is the case in
most Western nations, but the numbers for Iceland are still high, especially
among those who take sport seriously (see Figure 3.1). Those numbers show
that over 40% of Icelandic adolescents (14–15 year-olds) practice sport in
a sports club four times a week or more (Halldorsson, 2014). These figures
are higher than in most other European countries (see van Tuyckom, 2016).
Icelandic children generally practice multi-sports (i.e., take part in different
sports), at least until their teenage years.

Since the sports clubs are community based, they do not exclude those
who lack the skills to become accomplished players. Everyone interested
in participating gets to play, at least until they enter the senior age group at
the age of 20. As the clubs are based on the work of volunteers they try to
maintain broad membership. Some provide opportunities for those not good
enough to play with the higher-rated teams to play in lower league teams –
more for fun than for establishing a career in sport. The clubs also acknowledge that mass participation in youth sports provides them with social
capital. Former participants become volunteers. They engage in the day-to-
day activity of the clubs: serving on committees, helping with fund-raising

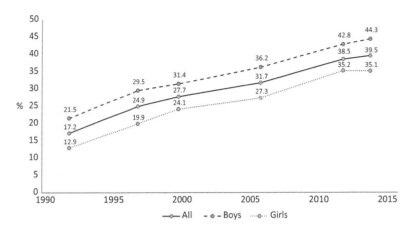

Figure 3.1 Adolescent participation in formal sports in Iceland; those who practice four times a week or more within sport clubs (see Halldorsson, 2014)

and becoming referees or supporters. In 2009, around 45% of the Icelandic population (150,000 people) were registered in a sports club within the National Olympic and Sports Association (Þórlindsson et al., 2015).

Football is the most popular sport in Iceland, with about 23,000 registered participants (see Table 3.1). Football is followed by golf with about 18,000 participants, gymnastics with 13,000, horseback riding with 11,000, handball with 8,000, basketball with around 7,000 and badminton with 5,500.[5]

These participation numbers show that only about 6,300 over the age of 16 were involved in football, 2,500 in handball and 3,000 in basketball; further analysis of the figures by gender show that about 1,500 Icelandic men practice handball and around 2,200 practice basketball (not shown in Table 3.1). These figures give an indication of the scale of Icelandic sports; the numbers reflect the pool from which the national teams have to select their players. For comparison, in Norway, which has a population of around five million, over 360,000 people play football, 114,000 play handball and about 100,000 play basketball (Norges Idrettsforbund, 2013, 65). Thus, the Norwegian national teams have 12–15 times more players to choose from for their national teams in sports than Iceland.

Sports furthermore have a high general status and a strong following in the community. Kuper and Szymanski, for instance, argue that Iceland is "the most football-loving country in Europe," where the viewing figures for the 2010 World Cup were highest in Iceland among the European nations – even though Iceland was not participating in the tournament (2014: 256–259).

Table 3.1 Registered participants in formal sports within the federations under the
National Olympic and Sports Association in 2014[1]

Sport	Total Participants	Male	Female	<15 yrs.	>16 yrs.
Football	22,638	15,421	7,217	16,284	6,354
Golf	17,772	12,457	5,315	1,502	16,270
Gymnastics	13,138	4,334	8,804	12,247	891
Equestrian	10,998	5,634	5,364	2,811	8,187
Handball	8,221	5,069	3,152	5,765	2,456
Basketball	6,782	4,780	2,002	3,785	2,997
Badminton	5,521	3,166	2,355	2,574	2,947
Track and field	4,982	2,343	2,639	3,274	1,708
Shooting	4,304	4,026	278	3	4,301
Volleyball	3,149	1,068	2,081	737	2,412
Swimming	3,108	1,349	1,759	2,593	515
Dance	2,777	873	1,904	1,477	1,300
Motor sports	2,167	1,915	252	155	2,012
Tennis	1,697	971	726	405	1,292
Karate	1,493	1,078	415	1,128	365
Fencing	1,333	941	392	267	1,066
Skiing	1,295	1,071	224	142	1,153
Sailing	1,256	659	597	922	334
Weight lifting	1,252	899	353	29	1,223
Judo	1,016	900	166	571	495
Other	18,7333	11,570	7,113	7,242	11,441
Total:	**133,632**	**80,524**	**53,108**	**63,913**	**69,719**

1 Official data from the National Olympic and Sports Association (ÍSÍ). Available online at:
www.isi.is/library/Skrar/Efnisveita/Tolfraedi/2013/lðkendur%202014%20eftir%20%C3%
ADþróttagreinum.pdf?=

Audience rankings of live coverage of Iceland's national team games on television rate among the highest in the history of Icelandic television. For instance, around 82% of the population watched Iceland play Denmark in the men's competition in the 2010 European handball championship.[6] On the day the team arrived back in Iceland with their Olympic medals a welcoming reception in the heart of the capital, Reykjavik, attracted over 40,000 spectators – around 12% of the population. Icelandic supporters bought 27,000 tickets for Iceland's matches in the Men's European Championship finals in 2016 – the equivalent of over 8% of the Icelandic population going to France to watch the team play. Corresponding figures based on the same percentage for Germany and England would be 6.6 million and 4.4 million supporters, respectively.[7] Those who stayed at home watched the matches Iceland played on television: 99% of all those who were watching television on the Sunday when Iceland played against Hungary, at the group stage, were watching the match. After the championship, tens of thousands of Icelanders welcomed the team back home in a big celebration in downtown Reykjavik.

Such figures indicate the genuine interest Icelanders have in the participation of their national teams in international sporting competitions – at least when they do well. Part of this interest lies in the nation's collective consciousness, which functions as social capital for those teams (see further in Chapter 9). When the teams play – and do well – it becomes something more than sport alone: they make Icelanders proud because they project their national identity.

The amateur nature of Icelandic sports

Historically the Nordic nations have placed great emphasis on amateurism in sport and also on socialization through sport (Jørgensen, 1998, 93). However, while sports in the Scandinavian countries has moved rapidly towards professionalism since the 1980s (Anderson and Ronglan, 2012), Icelandic sports can still be characterized by the amateur ethos. As noted above, Icelandic sports clubs are organized by voluntary organizations open to everybody. This attachment to voluntary associations has always been the case in Iceland. In 1982 Icelandic sport historian Ingimar Jónsson wrote: "The Icelandic people have always considered themselves as amateurs in sport and it's often stated that Icelanders are the only amateurs in the world" (1982, 21).

Sports in Iceland are in part funded by the state and municipalities. The state finances *the National Olympic and Sports Association (ISI)*, several sports funds and school sports – among other things – through the Ministry of Education, Science and Culture. The municipalities support their sports clubs financially and offer sports facilities for the clubs and the local community. The municipalities play a much larger role than the state in the funding of the sports clubs (Þórlindsson et al., 2015).

The clubs employ full-time staff, who handle their day-to-day running[8], and also coaches for all ages – who mostly work part-time. However, Icelandic sports clubs are still built on the work of volunteers at the community level. Basketball coach Steinþórsson says: "there would be no sports in Iceland if the parents and ex-athletes were not involved in it on a voluntary basis." Several researchers have argued that the volunteers are the driving force behind the sport clubs (Gísladóttir, 2006; Hrafnsdóttir, Jónsdóttir and Kristmundsson, 2014).

The sports system in Iceland is grounded in such community-level organizations, which have based their work on the notion of amateurism. Iceland does not host professional sports leagues and the structure and ideology of formal competitive sports in Iceland depart in some ways from how sports are pursued in larger nations. It could be argued that Icelandic sports are based on a sports-for-all philosophy. Participation in the clubs is open to everyone and fees are relatively low. The clubs are non-profit organizations and the participation fees are intended to cover the expenses of coaches' salaries and the costs of day-to-day management

However, times are changing. Global professionalization of sports is altering modern sports (Maguire, 1999) and this is beginning to show in Iceland. The top football leagues are semi-professional: all players are under contract and receive a low fee for their commitment and services. However, most of the players also work full-time outside football or are in formal education. Players in the top leagues in handball and basketball are also under contract with their clubs, but their financial rewards are much smaller than in football. Players of other sports in Iceland are generally amateurs.

It could be argued that the youth sports system in Iceland is well established, due to the affluence of Icelandic society; in it, children and adolescents have the opportunity to practice organized sports under professional supervision in good facilities with the help of volunteer parents. However, elite sports in Iceland have been seriously underfunded. A report made by the National Olympic and Sports Association in 2015 (ÍSÍ, 2015) states that the environment in which Icelandic competitors develop is completely different from what other nations offer in major events. The report estimates that Icelandic elite sports need five times the sums that the states gives to sports to bring Iceland closer to what the other countries are doing.

A stark contrast can be seen between the financial capacity of the Icelandic elite sports establishment and that of their foreign competitors in major tournaments. The national teams work at the amateur level. For instance, before the 2012 Olympics, the Icelandic Handball Association provided the men's national team with only 7% of the financial backing that the Danish Handball Federation provided for its team, for the same competition (ÍSÍ, 2015). The members of the national gymnastics team had to save and pay for their traveling and expenses themselves when they competed in the European Championship Finals – which they eventually won, becoming Iceland's first adult European Championship team. Likewise the only Icelandic gymnast who qualified for the 2016 Olympic Games worked three jobs – cleaning hotel rooms, delivering pizzas and coaching children in gymnastics – while preparing for the Games.[9] This workload was not the case for her competitors at the Games. When the men's basketball team qualified for the European Championship finals for the first time in 2015, volunteers and patrons collected money so the team would be able to take part; basketball players do not receive any money for playing for the national team and the same goes for handball players. Veteran basketball player Bæringsson said: "I have paid my way

practically throughout my career. What keeps me in this is the company."
Although the national players are professional in the club teams, when playing for the national team – even in big tournaments such as European Championships and the Olympic Games – players in these sports can be regarded as amateurs.

The Icelandic national youth teams work at this level. For instance, members of all national youth teams (except football) have to raise funds to cover the expenses they have to pay for national team projects. They sell products such as toilet paper, wash cars and seek grants from companies and municipalities. In the end, most of the funding comes from their parents (ÍSÍ, 2015). Players in the youth handball teams even have to pay half of all of the expenses borne by Iceland of hosting international competitions in Iceland. Thus, they have to pay for accommodation, transport and meals for the visiting teams. This is also the case in most sports.

Financially, however, football is in a league of its own in Icelandic sports, due largely to the grants that the football associations receive from UEFA and FIFA and the massive participation in the sport. All expenses of the youth and A-team players are paid by the Icelandic Football Association (KSÍ). The A-team players receive bonus payments for winning games and the men's team received bonus payments for qualifying for the European Finals. However, the amounts that Icelandic players receive are far lower than those paid to players from other countries. It can be argued that the Icelandic national teams managed to do well in those top international sports competitions without the financial resources of most – if not all – of their opponents. The long-time Icelandic Handball Association secretary-general, Einar Þorvarðarson, wondered "How have we managed to achieve all we have done with so little money?"[10] The financial handicap the sports associations have been facing – compared to their opponents – makes the case of the Icelandic national teams even more intriguing.

In the next chapters I will demonstrate more specifically how the Icelandic sports culture – described above – played a key role in the development of Iceland's athletes and the achievements of the Icelandic national teams in question.

Notes

1 "Icelanders have long lived on dreams" (article, *ft.com*, 2016, June). See: https://www.ft.com/content/f0a87fde-3bb2-11e6-8716-a4a71e8140b0.
2 In this formative period, sport was predominantly organized by males for males in Iceland, as in other countries.
3 Academics who have studied the Nordic sports model have left Iceland out of the analysis (see for instance Bairner, 2010; Meinander and Mangan, 1998). Thus, the nuances and peculiarities of Icelandic sports, in relation to the Nordic sports model, have not been addressed in the literature to date.

36   *Setting the scene*

4 "Við erum íþróttabrjálað fólk" (article; *Mbl.is.*, 2015, October). See: www.mbl.
   is/vidskipti/frettir/2015/10/08/vid_erum_ithrottabrjalad_folk/
5 Official figures from the Icelandic Olympic and Sport Association (ÍSÍ). See:
   www.isi.is/library/Skrar/Efnisveita/Tolfraedi/2013/Iðkendur%202014%20
   eftir%20%C3%AÐþróttagreinum.pdf?=
6 "Sjónvarpsáhorf: Þýskaland 10%, Austurríki 14, Ísland 99" (article; *Visir.is.*, 2010,
   January). See: www.visir.is/sjonvarpsahorf – thyskaland-10-prosent,-austurriki-
   14,-island-99/article/2010810634157
7 "Iceland fans flood to apply for EURO tickets" (article; *Uefa.com.*, 2016, January).
   See: www.uefa.com/uefaeuro/news/newsid=2325211.html
8 The staff in the Icelandic sports movement work the usual eight hours per day but due
   to the heavy workload it is not uncommon that they add extra hours to their jobs without
   pay, which can be labeled as volunteer work. "Einar Þorvarðarson: Enginn oflaunaður
   í íslensku íþróttahreyfingunni" (article; Fimmeinn.is., 2017, January). See: www2.
   fimmeinn.is/einar-thorvardarson-enginn-oflaunadur-i-islensku-ithrottahreyfingunni/
9 Ruv.is "Ólympíufari keyrir út pizzur og þrífur hótel. (article; *Ruv.is.*, 2016, July).
   See: www.ruv.is/frett/olympiufari-keyrir-ut-pizzur-og-thrifur-hotel
10 "Einar: Maður spyr sig hvernig við náðum öllum þessum árangri" (article; *Visir.is.*,
   2016, July). See: www.visir.is/einar-madur-spyr-sig-hvernig-vid-nadum-ollum-
   thessum-arangri/article/2016160728895

References

Anderson, S.S. and Ronglan, L.T. (eds.) (2012). *Nordic elite sport: Same ambitions, different tracks*. Oslo: Universitetsforlaget.

Bairner, A. (2010). What is Scandinavian about Scandinavian Sport? *Sport in Society*, 13(4): 734–743.

Bjarnason, B. (1908). *Íþróttir fornmanna á Norðurlöndum*. Reykjavík: Sigurður Kristjánsson.

Crum, B.J. (1991). *Over Versporting vand de Samenleving*. Rijswijk: WVC.

Elias, N. and Dunning, E. (1986). *Quest for excitement: Sport and leisure in the civilizing process*. London: Wiley-Blackwell.

Finnbogason, G. ([1933]/1971). *Íslendingar: Nokkur drög að þjóðarlýsingu*. Reykjavík: Almenna Bókafélagið.

Gísladóttir, Þ. (2006). *Hagrænt gildi íþrótta í íslensku nútímasamfélagi*. Unpublished MA dissertation from Bifröst University, Iceland.

Halldorsson, V. (2014). *Íþróttaþátttaka íslenskra ungmenna: Þróun og helstu áhrifaþættir*. *Netla*, 20 December. Available online at: http://netla.hi.is/greinar/2014/ryn/007.pdf

Hrafnsdóttir, S., Jónsdóttir, G.A. and Kristmundsson, Ó.H. (2014). Þátttaka í sjálfboðaliðastarfi á Íslandi. *Stjórnmál og Stjórnsýsla*, 10(2): 427–444.

ÍSÍ (2015). *Kostnaður vegna afreksíþróttastarfs á Íslandi*. Reykjavík: ÍSÍ.

Jónsson, I. (1982). *Íþróttir og samfélag*. Reykjavík: Menntamálaráðuneytið.

Jónsson, I. (1983). *Ágrip af sögu íþrótta: Ísland*. Reykjavík: Menntamálaráðuneytið.

Jónsson, J. (1906). *Gullöld Íslendinga: Menning og lífshættir feðra vorra á söguöldinni*. Reykjavík: Sigurður Kristjánsson.

Jørgensen, P. (1998). From Balck to Nurmi: The Olympic movement and the Nordic nations. In H. Meinander and J.A. Mangan (eds.), *The Nordic world: Sport in society* (pp. 69–99). London: Frank Cass.

Karlsson, G. (1995). The emergence of nationalism in Iceland. In S. Tägil (ed.), *Ethnicity and nation building in the Nordic world* (pp. 33–65). Carbondale, IL: Southern Illinois University Press.

Kuper, S. and Szymansky, S. (2014). *Soccernomics*. London: HarperSport.

Loftsdottir, K. (2015). Vikings invade present-day Iceland. In E.P. Durrenberger and G. Palsson (eds.), *Gambling debt: Iceland's rise and fall in the global economy* (pp. 3–14). Boulder: University Press of Colorado.

Maguire, J. (1999). *Global sport: Identities, societies, civilizations*. Cambridge: Polity.

Meinander, H. (1998). Prologue: Nordic history, society and sport. In H. Meinander and J.A. Mangan (eds.), *The Nordic world: Sport in society* (pp. 1–10). London: Frank Cass.

Meinander, H. and Mangan, J.A. (1998). *The Nordic world: Sport in society*. London: Frank Cass.

Mixa, M.W. and Vaiman, V. (2015). Individualistic Vikings: Culture, economics and Iceland. *Icelandic Review of Politics and Administration*, 11(2): 355–374.

Norges Idrettsforbund (2013). *Årsrapport 2013*. Available online at: www.idretts forbundet.no/globalassets/idrett/idrettsforbundet/om-nif/arsrapporter/aarsrap port2013.pdf

Tuyckom, C. van (2016). A comparison between European member states. In K. Green and A. Smith (eds.), *Routledge handbook of youth sport* (pp. 61–71). London: Routledge.

Valgeirsson, G. (1991). *Sport in Iceland: A case study of the voluntary sport movement*. PhD. thesis from Bowling Green State University.

Wieting, S. (2015). *The sociology of hypocrisy: An analysis of sport and religion*. London: Routledge.

Þórlindsson, Þ., Halldórsson, V., Hallgrímsson, H., Lárusson, D. and Geirs, D.P. (2015). *Íþróttir á Íslandi: Umfang og hagræn áhrif*. Reykjavík: Félagsvísindastofnun Háskóla Íslands.

Þórlindsson, Þ., Karlsson, Þ. and Sigfúsdóttir, I.D. (1992). *Um gildi íþrótta fyrir íslensk ungmenni*. Reykjavík: RUM.

Þórlindsson, Þ., Sigfúsdóttir, I.D., Bernburg, J.G. and Halldórsson, V. (1997). *Vímuefnaneysla ungs fólks: Umhverfi og aðstæður*. Reykjavík: RUM.

Þórlindsson, Þ., Sigfúsdóttir, I.D., Halldórsson, V. and Ólafsson, K. (2000). *Félagsstarf og frístundir íslenskra ungmenna*. Reykjavík: Æskan.

Part II

How Icelandic sports progressed

4 Building the infrastructure
Towards professionalism

Progress is impossible without change.

– George Bernard Shaw

The general sports culture in Iceland in the late twentieth century was not well suited to provide Iceland with the right ingredients to produce teams that could qualify for the top international championships and compete among the best teams in the world. Icelandic teams had achieved some impressive individual results but lacked the (collective) consistency to make any real impact in international sports. The teams were vulnerable to big failures, resulting in humiliating defeats. For instance, Icelanders grieved when the men's football team lost 14:2 against Denmark in 1967. In this context, the historian and former sports journalist, Steinar J. Lúðvíksson, recalls the anxiety of covering Icelandic teams in the late twentieth century:

> I was a sports reporter for many years and I was always on tenterhooks. Worried that we would be hammered. We had it in our subconscious all the time that we were inferior. Hoped we might get by and lose by not too much . . . it's all completely different now.

With the exception of the men's handball team, no Icelandic national team qualified for a major championship until 2008. This demonstrates that a general cultural change was needed for Icelandic sports to reach new heights and succeed in other sports apart from handball. These changes gradually took place.

The establishment of a successful sports tradition in Iceland did not happen all at once; it has developed in spurts, and to a different degree in different sports at different times (see Thorlindsson and Halldorsson, 2017). But it is the emergence of this tradition that provided younger generations with the premises, resources and the "cultural toolkits" (see Swidler, 1986) that enabled Iceland to take a leap forward in international sports. Thus, it is appropriate to give an account of the development of sports in Iceland towards professionalism and how achievements of the aforementioned national teams, in recent years, rest on those developments.

Icelandic sporting organizations have made important steps towards professionalism since the 1980s. According to Líney Halldórsdóttir, secretary-general of the National Olympic and Sports Association, one important step was the merger of the Icelandic Sports Association and the Olympic Committee in 1997. She argues:

> I think the merger of the Association and the Olympic Committee helped to make things more professional. It was then that we started working with a professional team and setting out demands to the specialist federations. Made it a requirement that each federation was to have its achievement policy and so on.

The governing bodies started to aim at long-term goals and to implement strategy that would benefit them in the long run. One of these goals involved giving Icelandic athletes more international experience, with this implementation of strategy in mind. The specific strategy involved efforts on the part of the National Sports Association to send as many athletes to the Olympic Games as possible. Many of them managed this under "B" qualifications, with little or no realistic chance of doing anything spectacular at the Games, but they would gain important experience for their future careers.

The degree to which sports clubs started to take coaching seriously constituted another important step forward in the late twentieth century. Until the early 1980s, coaching was a hobby in Iceland. Anton Bjarnason, who was then a teacher in the Sports Education School in Iceland, remembers when sport clubs started to contact him and ask whether there were any coaches they could hire for the summer. This proactive search for coaches soon became the norm in Icelandic youth sports. Later, an emphasis on paid and specialized coaches started to evolve, and today all participants, from the beginning of their sports participation – from the age of four – are coached by paid, and most often educated, coaches. Iceland differs in this way from most other European nations, where parents tend to coach the younger children.

In recent years, great emphasis has been placed on coaches' education in Icelandic sports, particularly in football. Through the initiative of the Football Association, Iceland now has far more coaches with UEFA coaching certificates, per capita, than its neighboring countries. The numbers of educated football coaches are "figures you don't see in other countries," says Sigurður Ragnar Eyjólfsson. Although there has been growing emphasis on providing good coaches at all levels of sport in Iceland, other sporting federations apart from football have not attached such importance to coaches' own training and qualifications.

It has also been argued that accessibility to suitable sports facilities and the general quality of such facilities has been another important factor for Iceland's achievements, especially in team sports.[1] Historically, the practice of winter sports such as handball and basketball takes place in the local indoor sports halls because of the long and cold winters in Iceland. These halls were first built in the late twentieth century in connection with schools and the local sport clubs all around the country and are today usually well-equipped and modern. The locally situated indoor halls played a part in the development of handball in the middle of the twentieth century and helped it to gain its status as Iceland's national sport (Lúðvíksson, 2012). One of the benefits of living in a small society, with a wide range of locally situated sports facilities, is that distances between key areas of action are usually short. People in such communities tend to spend less time traveling to and from work, and children can usually walk or bike to school or to the sports club.

Children go to practice or "hang out" in the sports halls (Halldorsson, Thorlindsson and Katovich, 2014), as do volunteers and other enthusiasts. The community sport clubs are ideally always open to all their members – especially in smaller towns and villages around Iceland. The halls have proved important for indoor sports such as handball and basketball. Handball player Gústafsson noted: "We had those halls; we had all the facilities. Just like football has got all its facilities in place these last few years. In our dark winters we couldn't play football all year."

Football became an all-year sport in the late 1990s. Until then it was customary in the multi-sport environment to have the main focus on indoor sports, such as handball and basketball, during the winter and on summer sports, like football, during the summer. Over the past few decades, football has been played outside all year round in Iceland. This change was in part initiated by the introduction of artificial grass fields, making it possible to play outdoors in the wintertime.

Since the turn of the century, special indoor football halls with artificial grass have begun to spring up where football can be played indoors all year round. One of the male football players, Finnbogason, recognized the importance of the indoor hall where he grew up:

> I reckon my generation is the first that reaped the benefit of the football halls. I remember when Egilshöllin was opened in Grafarvogur, where I lived. I was 10 or 11 at the time and to be able to practice there was a huge change.

The surprising improvement in the quality of the national football teams in recent years, and their successes, have been attributed to the coming of these indoor football halls. However, the importance of the halls for the achievements of the current national teams has been overstated. Analysis reveals that only a handful of the players on the men's football team played in clubs that possessed indoor football halls in their formative years.[2] Most of the players did not have the opportunity to practice in such halls on a regular basis.

Thus, there are various structural factors in the organization of sports in Iceland – such as improved infrastructure, better coaching and appropriate sports facilities – that have contributed to progress in recent years. Nevertheless, Iceland had to rely on foreign expertise as well as opportunities and trends in global sports to develop further.

Global influences: expertise and opportunities

At the beginning of the twentieth century, the Icelandic Olympic wrestler Sigurjón Pétursson wrote: "We make virtually no progress in sports because we don't benefit from our practicing – we don't know how to do it properly" (Muller, 1911, VII). The isolation of Iceland – as an island in the Atlantic Ocean – had reinforced existing views, values and methods that Icelanders were accustomed to. Such a state of affairs leads to stagnation and deterioration of results in international comparison, which for instance was the case in the men's football team in the 2000s. The spark of progress for Icelandic sports, however, lies in the increased promotion of new ideas and new methods of how to do things – which Icelanders were not accustomed to – as a by-product of globalization in the late twentieth century. It took foreign influences and expertise to stimulate the Icelandic way of doing things and helped steer Iceland in the direction of more systematic and professional ways of approaching sports.

The influx of foreign coaches

The first relevant impact of global expertise for Icelandic sports comes with the influx of foreign coaches to Iceland, bringing with them new ideas and ways of doing things, based on a different mindset and methods of training that differed from what Icelanders were used to. Some of these coaches came to revolutionize how Icelanders played sport.

Of the Icelandic national teams, as mentioned before, the handball team has the longest history of good results in international competitions. Handball gained an earlier advantage from the presence of foreign coaches than did football and basketball. World-class foreign coaches, mainly from Eastern Europe, started coming into Icelandic handball in the 1970s and

soon started to make their mark. It was in many ways fortunate for Icelandic handball that emphasis was on foreign coaches rather than players
(see Guðbjartsson, 2012, 267). "We were very much open to new things,
to looking at things from outside. An example of this is how we had foreign coaches coming here, something that was not common in Denmark,
for example," said the Icelandic handball coach Gudmundur Gudmunds-
son. A Pole, Janus Zerwinsky, was appointed national team coach in 1976,
and two years later he encouraged his friend, another Polish coach, Bogdan
Kowalczyk, to come to Iceland. Bodgan became the coach of Víkingur (a
club in Reykjavik) and the national team coach in 1983.

Bodgan Kowalczyk has in fact been named as the key person in the transformation of Icelandic handball in the late twentieth century. The approach and
methods he proposed were, at that time, unknown in Icelandic sports. Guðmundur Guðmundsson was a player under Bogdan at that time. He recalls:

The feeling I had was that something really interesting was going on
there, something about how he approached his work as a coach. In my
opinion he raised Icelandic handball up to a new level. I think having
him was one of the biggest factors in transforming Icelandic handball.

Kowalczyk brought with him a professional attitude that had been unknown
in Icelandic handball up to that time. He instilled in his players the understanding that they had to invest substantially more in their sport in order to
reach higher levels and achieve something special. He took the volume and
intensity of training up a level and dragged the Icelandic amateurs out of
their comfort zone. Everything was organized. His methods were contro-
versial to begin with because to the Icelanders they seemed more like hard
physical labor – or military workouts – than play, which was something
that they, as amateurs, did not fancy. When the team started to improve and
get better results, Kowalczyk started to harvest respect, and other coaches
began to take notice of his philosophy and methods of more systematic
training. He was then appointed national team coach and took the national
team to new heights. Bogdan Kowalczyk brought a new dimension, and a
new way of thinking, into Icelandic handball in the 1980s.

Another foreign handball coach from Russia, Boris Akbachev, also had
great effect on the handball culture in Iceland. Akbachev was a master in
teaching and improving players' technical skills. Iceland's most distinguished handball player, Ólafur Stefánsson, used a metaphor of a ballet
dancer in describing the impact Boris had on the players in Iceland:

Say you were a ballet dancer. And you had an Icelandic woman coaching you, a woman who herself had stopped dancing when she was 25.

So she's teaching you something and you are just dancing like this, always making some moves. But every move is full of holes. And you go on and on, sort of like a Swiss cheese. Then 10 years later you've developed a certain pattern, ticked in all the boxes, but each box is really weak. That's what they were doing. As I realised through Boris, the basic technique was like what you see among good dancers. You don't go up to the next level until you've learned the basics thoroughly. He filled in all the gaps in our technique. You can see who's been through this school and who hasn't.

Foreign coaches such as Kowalczyk and Akbachev were highly influential for the transformation of Icelandic handball after the 1980s. They coached a golden generation of players who reached new heights in Icelandic handball. They furthermore influenced the next generation of Icelandic coaches, who in turn became highly successful in international handball.[3]

Similar experiences of the importance of foreign coaches apply to Icelandic basketball. For instance, in the 1990s a Hungarian basketball coach, Dr. Lazlo Nemeth, came to Iceland and some argue that he changed the mentality of Icelandic basketball the same way as Kowalczyk and Akbachev did for Icelandic handball. Nemeth, also an East European, put the focus on spending more time on training as well as more structure and organization in the Icelandic team than they were used to. "He didn't want to win games 95–90; he wanted to win 55–50," recalls Steinþórsson, one of his former players, emphasizing the coach's attention to better organization of his teams on the basketball court. Nemeth coached and influenced many of the coaches in Iceland who were responsible later on for building up the generation of Icelandic players who contributed the core of the national team that qualified for the European Championship in 2015. Two more foreign coaches have had a great influence on the progress of men's basketball in recent years. The Swede Peter Öqvist took over as head coach in 2012 and applied more professional methods to team training and also influenced the organization of the basketball federation. According to basketball player Stefánsson:

> It was all more "pro." He saw all these little things, for example making sure there wasn't someone walking across the field talking on his phone while we were training. Everything concerned with the team. He sifted through it all. I felt, and everyone felt, that this was a new beginning.

A Canadian, Craig Pedersen, pursued the work when he took over the men's team in 2014 and steered it to the European finals for the first time in 2015. The team had established new norms of training and playing and qualified again for the 2017 European finals.

Meanwhile, Icelandic football was slowly progressing in this direction, but such a dramatic change in the football sports culture – as had taken place particularly in handball – did not happen until the Swede Lars Lagerbäck took over the men's national team in 2011. The experienced Lagerbäck – who had coached Sweden and Nigeria in major international competitions – instilled more professionalism into the Icelandic national team and also into the Icelandic Football Federation. Like the other foreign coaches named above, he brought more systematic methods and way of playing to the team and its surroundings. The structure and organization of the team, and its preparation for matches, improved considerably. One of the players, Kolbeinn Sigþórsson, said:

> Training sessions with him [Lars] aren't always that enjoyable. . . . But we can't whine about this and about not being allowed to go out onto the pitch and play every time in practice. It's more important to get the team to work together and brush up our tactics in defence and attack."[4]

The team started to focus on its strengths, its defensive play, which breathed confidence into the players. This was achieved through discipline and professional attitude and trust in the players. One of the football players, Gunnleifsson, who played in the team both before and after the appointment of Lars Lagerbäck, noted the difference in team culture in this way:

> We came into the hotel to meet the lads, have fun and be members of the national team. The practices were built on sloppy tradition. It's all much more professional now. The coaches have all the practices carefully organized. We have to do exactly the training that we need to do.

Lagerbäck's impact on the national football team was based on a more general professional attitude towards everything that had to do with the sport than had existed before. Changes were made in the Icelandic Football Association, as well as in the preparation of the team and how it trained, traveled and prepared itself for games. These ideas were different from what preceded them and they were far more constructive.

Only a few of the foreign coaches who came to work in Iceland are mentioned above. Lagerbäck was the right man at the right time for Icelandic football, just as Bogdan Kowalczyk was for Icelandic handball and Peter Öqvist and Craig Pedersen were for Icelandic basketball. Many others also made important contributions to Icelandic sports, influencing athletes, coaches, and sporting organizations and adding important professional knowledge to Icelandic sports in general.

Players' migration

Iceland is not a member of the European Union, but since 1994 it has been a participant in European cooperation by being a member of the European Economic Area (EEA). This Europe-ization has led to increased cooperation between Iceland and other European nations in various spheres, which has influenced Icelandic society in profound ways (Bergmann, 2005). This cooperative arrangement also affects sports. Increased labor migration – which in sport was spurred by the Bosman ruling in football (in 1995) and led to the abandonment of a quota system of foreign players in European sport leagues (Magee and Sugden, 2002) – paved the way for unrestricted transfers of players from one European country to another. This provided athletes from Iceland with increased opportunities to play professionally abroad (Magnusson, 2001), where they were introduced to the norms and customs of professional elite sports.

Some scholars have argued that national teams that contain higher percentages of players playing in professional leagues outside their own country perform better than others (Baur and Lehmann, 2008; Frick, 2009). This has at least turned out to be particularly beneficial for Iceland. Since the 1990s, the number of Icelandic professional players has multiplied (see Magnusson, 2001). Player migrations (both to and from Iceland) have facilitated a flow of sporting knowledge and expertise between the professional worlds of sports outside the country and the amateur sports scene in Iceland. Today the players in the national teams expect the same professionalism in their national teams as they are used to in their professional club teams abroad. Football staff member Þráinsson's example of the men's football team further shows the importance of professionalism in all areas: "These guys are used to the bus coming at exactly the right time, breakfast is there on the minute, there are always balls and the goals are always in the right place." This emphasis on specific goals and methods is the case for all the different national teams in question, which in turn illustrates the increased professionalism as a general trend in Icelandic sports.

The increased international experience of the younger players led not only to more professional attitudes on their part but also humanized the great foreign players and the big teams in their eyes, leading to greater self-confidence. Former handball player and sports broadcaster Einar Örn Jónsson says:

> All the mystique about foreigners who never make a mistake, it disappears when you play with them and get to know them. When you beat them, in club teams or European matches. You don't always have to win these games, but you see: 'I can beat him' . . . Handball was

where this happened first, with players going professional and having their eyes opened. 'These guys are the best in the world, but I'm just as good.' Then you start to believe that you can beat them. This has become the general, accepted attitude in Icelandic team sports. When you go to play a match, you go with the idea that you can win if you do your best.

This view was shared by many of the interviewed athletes. Bæringsson, a senior basketball player, shares his experiences of the change in belief:

> The guys in the team also got more experience. More chances to play in Europe. It wasn't such a big thing. They saw where this one and that one from the other teams were playing. When more of us were playing in Europe, it all became closer to us. And our opponents weren't automatically on a pedestal; they became equals in a way. That was how this change in attitude came about, slowly but surely.

Most of the key players in the Icelandic men's football team went abroad to play professionally in their late adolescence. They had been built and formed, in their younger years, from the strong youth sport system in Iceland and then, as they became older, they were introduced to a more professional environment. It could be argued that they "got the best of both worlds" in this sense. One of the female football players describes her experiences when she turned professional as follows: "I found myself bumping into lots and lots of walls when I started out as a professional abroad, even though I had had a very successful career here in Iceland. It's just that the standard over there is so much higher."[5]

Some socio-cultural and economic dynamics must be examined further in this context. Due to the lack of financial resources in the Icelandic amateur sporting leagues, Icelandic sports teams have been keen to sell their players to professional teams abroad – often at a very low price. It is custom that teams don't stand in the way of the dreams of players who want to try their luck playing professionally abroad. It is important here that the smooth flow of player transfers from Iceland to professional clubs abroad had favorable unanticipated consequences for Icelandic sports (see Merton, 1996, 173–182).

First, the players gained important knowledge and expertise from playing professional sports, which they could not acquire in the amateur leagues in Iceland, expertise that benefits not only themselves and their careers but also other Icelandic players and the Icelandic national teams. A handball player, Stefánsson, noted how the more experienced players influenced other national team members in various ways, such as how to practice and take care of their bodies (see further in Chapter 9).

A second unanticipated consequence for Icelandic sports, in this context of increased players' migration, involves the necessity of Icelandic sporting leagues to rely more on younger Icelandic players and has thus provided a window of opportunity for young players to train and play with adults at the top level in Iceland. This has been beneficial for younger Icelandic athletes, who gain important trial-and-error experience of playing the game with adults from early on. Handball player Stefánsson emphasizes the importance of such educational experiments for young athletes, as he uses a metaphor of a chemist to illustrate the point of craftsmanship as an important approach to learning (see Sennett, 2008):

> This chemist has been in the system for five years and has learnt everything about chemicals, but has never handled them. Which way is better? Should you blow up your workshed first? That was my experience, and maybe that's the good thing about Iceland. You get to play around a bit and try a bit of everything.

It is not unusual to see young players playing for the Icelandic Premier league teams in football, handball and basketball, filling the gap which those players who have left Iceland to play professionally abroad. This reliance on youth is especially evident in women's sports, where young girls are brought into the adult teams early on due to the limited number of women in those sports compared to the high number of teams.

Global sporting politics

The third important impact of global influences on Icelandic sports is related to sporting politics. Iceland has benefitted from important decisions and strategies made in global sporting politics: first, by systematic changes in the organization of major sporting contests. Iceland, like other small nations, has had to rely on favorable decisions taken at the top levels of these organizations. Increased numbers of participating nations in the top tournaments have provided other nations – other than the "usual suspects" – better chances to compete on the largest stage. The number of nations that qualify for the men's European Football Championship finals was increased from 20 to 24 in 2016[6] – providing the Icelandic team with a more realistic chance to qualify for the tournament – and in turn a stronger motivation to do so. This was also the case in women's football, where in 1997 the number of nations that qualified for the finals rose from four to eight; it is set to rise still further, to 16, in 2017. This has also been the case in basketball. The European Basketball Association recently made important changes to its system, at the initiative of the chairman at the time, the Icelander Ólafur

Rafnsson. This increased the chances of small nations to qualify for the European Championship finals. Steinþórsson described it like this:

> Then changes were made to the system. The way it used to be, they made sure that the big nations got in. Then it was changed to a group-stage competition like in football. It gives small countries better chances, and we got in at the second attempt. After the first, we could see there was a chance there for us.

Nevertheless, the larger nations have a tendency to try to control the organization of sports in a way that benefits them over teams from smaller countries. It is best, both financially and as regards global prestige, for the largest countries' teams to play each other. For instance, in the last two decades, the top European football teams wanted to establish a Super League so they could play each other more often.[7] Eggert Magnússon, former President of the Icelandic Football Association, acknowledges that these attempts were made in UEFA, but – fortunately for Iceland – without success.

Finally, also part of global sport politics, increased funding from the professional sports world has proved to be very important for Icelandic sports in recent years. Increased funding has in particular been the case in the field of football, but to a much lesser degree in other sports. The large international football sports federations, UEFA and FIFA, have increasingly transferred funding to their national member federations, based in part on how successful the member states are. For a small nation such as Iceland – with a very small economy – this has been a massive boost for the Icelandic Football Association and the football clubs (see Þórlindsson et al., 2015). Eggert Magnússon reflects on how this works in Iceland:

> When we started making a profit and got more and more from UEFA and FIFA, then we put this money into the clubs. The total sums are not huge, but they make it easier for the clubs to develop.

The increased funding has helped to build better infrastructure, particularly in relation to coaches' education and the development of sports facilities in Iceland.

Notes

1 "Iceland: How a country with 329.000 people reached Euro 2016" (article; *Bbc. com.*, 2015, November). See: www.bbc.com/sport/football/30012357
2 "Gerðu hallirnar Frakklandshetjurnar virkilega svona góðar?" (article, *Frettatiminn.is.*, 2016, July). See: www.frettatiminn.is/wp-content/uploads/2016/07/02 07_2016_LR.pdf (p. 8).

3 Today, Icelandic coaches are recognized throughout the handball world and they coach some of the best teams in the world. For instance, in 2015, Icelandic coaches were voted the best in the world in men's and women's handball by the International Handball Federation See: "Two Icelanders on the top: Sigurdsson and Hergeirsson elected Coach of the year 2015" (article; *Ihf.info.*, 2016, April). See: www.ihf.info/en-us/mediacentre/news/newsdetails.aspx?ID=3158
4 "Stundum leiðinlegt á æfingum hjá Lars" (article; *Visir.is.*, 2015, October). See: www.visir.is/stundum-leidinlegt-a-aefingum-hja-lars/article/2015151008619
5 Whether it is good for very young players to go abroad to play professional sport is another question that won't be discussed here.
6 The FIFA World Cup will be expanded from 32 teams to 48 teams in 2026. See: www.fifa.com/about-fifa/news/y=2017/m=1/news=fifa-council-unanimously-decides-on-expansion-of-the-fifa-world-cuptm – 2863100.html?intcmp=fifacom_hp_module_news
7 "Stærstu lið Norðurlanda verða hluti af nýrri ofurdeild í Evrópu" (article; *Visir. is.*, 2016, October). See: www.visir.is/staerstu-lid-nordurlanda-verda-hluti-af-nyrri-ofurdeild-i-evropu/article/2016161019452

References

Bergmann, E. (2005). Evrópuvæðing Íslands. *Stjórnmál og Stjórnsýsla* (veftímarit), 1(1) 3–7.

Beur, D.G. and Lehmann, S. (2008). Does the mobility of football players influence the success of the national team? IIIS Discussion Paper, no. 217. Available online at SSRN: https://ssm.com/abstract=980936.

Frick, B. (2009). Globalization and factor mobility: The impact of the "Bosman-ruling" on player migration in professional soccer. *Journal of Sports Economics*, 10(1): 88–106.

Guðbjartsson, S. (2012). "Hverju vori fylgir sumar. . . ?" In S.J. Lúðvíksson (ed.), *Íþróttabókin: Saga og samfélag í 100 ár* (pp. 260–275). Reykjavík: ÍSÍ.

Halldorsson, V., Thorlindsson, T. and Katovich, M.A. (2014). The role of informal sport. The local context and the development of elite athletes. *Studies in Symbolic Interaction*, 42: 133–160.

Lúðvíksson, S.J. (ed.) (2012). *Íþróttabókin: Saga og samfélag í 100 ár*. Reykjavík: ÍSÍ.

Magee, J. and Sugden, J. (2002). "The world at their feet": Professional football and international labor migration. *Journal of Sport and Social Issues*, 26(4): 421–437.

Magnusson, G.K. (2001). The internalization of sports: The case of Iceland. *International Review for the Sociology of Sport*, 36(1): 59–69.

Merton, R.K. (1996). *On social structure and science*. Chicago: The University of Chicago Press.

Muller, J.P. (1911). *Mín aðferð*. Reykjavík: Sigurjón Pétursson & Pétur Halldórsson.

Sennett, R. (2008). *The craftsman*. New Haven: Yale University Press.

Swidler, A. (1986). Culture in action: Symbols and strategies. *American Sociological Review*, 51(2): 273–286.

Thorlindsson, T. and Halldorsson, V. (2017). The cultural production of a successful sport tradition: A case study of Icelandic handball. *Studies in Symbolic Interaction* (in press).

Þórlindsson, Þ., Halldórsson, V., Hallgrímsson, J.H., Lárusson, D. and Geirs, D.P. (2015). *Umfang og hagrænt gildi íþrótta: Áfangaskýrsla 2015*. Reykjavík: Félagsvísindastofnun Háskóla Íslands.

5 New conditions, new generation, new heights

The past does appear in the present.

– Edward Shils (1982, 35)

The culture of the former national teams of Iceland could in many ways be described as unprofessional, and organization and training were haphazard compared to today. These were just the norms of training and playing sport in Iceland at the time. Playing for the national team was, in a sense, like meeting and playing around with your friends, without the discipline and organization needed to do well in international sport. Thus, despite some good results and progress by the earlier Icelandic teams, a lack of discipline, accompanied by low self-confidence and an unprofessional culture, held them back for a long time. It was, for instance, common for team members to drink and party around national team sessions, as this confession from female football player Viðarsdóttir illustrates[1]:

> When I got into the national team, it was just a matter of trips to have parties. We went abroad somewhere, played a match and then came the party. That's how it was. Everyone was drunk and had a really good time

The parties were integral to the *esprit de corps* established in the team's ideo-cultures. The men's handball team had made some progress but it had difficulty accomplishing, collectively, what it set out to do in regards to advancing in tournaments – that is, winning a medal. One former handball player, Jónasson, noted: "It was always a question of doing better than the ones who had been there before us. If you improved on what they did, then you had done something. Earned your right to be stuck-up." Another former handball player, Jóhannesson, said:

> Maybe we had had enough. Maybe it was enough for us to get into the semi-finals as a team and get contracts with professional clubs as individuals. Maybe that was the top for us and we, our group, were satisfied with that.

The older generations had won their victories before, which were impressive in their own right. They had prestige in Icelandic sport and paved the way for the younger generations to follow their path and build on what they had achieved. With this foundation in place, the younger generation worked together to surpass previous achievements. However, the argument here is not that the younger generations built a brand new culture in those teams: they built on past traditions and incorporated the old with the new, leading to the new ideoculture. As Shils has argued: "What is new incorporates something of what preceded it even though it is a step on a path which leads away from the past in the present" (1982, 35). The recent Icelandic teams were based on the same collective enthusiasm and friendships as the former teams but in addition to that they were more professional, had more belief in themselves and aimed higher. Former international footballer Þorgrímur Þráinsson describes the difference between Icelandic sports today and in the past as "two different worlds." The former can be characterized by a culture of unprofessionalism where a lack of discipline and sports expertise hindered Icelandic teams from reaching their potential. Þráinsson further notes:

> The footballers I played with at that time [the 1980s] were no worse than the ones we have today. What was missing back then was the discipline and knowledge of the game, rest, diet and all the other things that are now in place.

Shils notes: "Having taken into them less of the past, new generations offer the chance of getting free of the grip of the past and to make a great leap forward" (1982, 36). This necessary freedom from the past is in fact illustrated to some extent in Icelandic sports. It took a new generation of Icelandic athletes, born between the early 1980s and the mid-1990s, to take the Icelandic national teams to new heights. The new generation was facilitated by the improved infrastructure and greater expertise in Icelandic sports, and hence came to possess better technical skills, and show a more professional attitude towards sports, than had their seniors. These added elements helped the Icelandic teams to burst onto the international scene (see the progress of the achievements of the Icelandic national teams in Figure 5.1).

It can be argued that the increased professionalism[2] of Icelandic sports in the late 1990s, and especially in the 2000s, benefitted the generation born between the early 1980s and the mid-1990s – sometimes referred to as "generation Y."[3] These younger Icelandic players received better coaching, practiced in better facilities and had more knowledge of how to behave professionally (for instance how to train more effectively and how to rest and eat) than did their seniors. Additionally, they had a more realistic chance of playing professionally abroad – often described as "every kid's dream" – fueling their ambition and motivation. The fresh, and more professional,

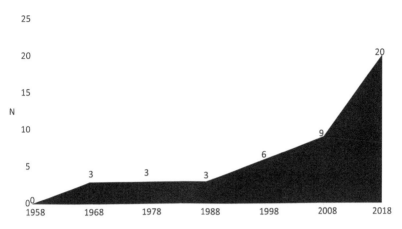

Figure 5.1 The number of Icelandic national teams that have qualified for major international competitions (in basketball, handball and football), in each decade, after the first in 1958

There are other influential factors that it is important to bear in mind in regard to Iceland's qualifications for major tournaments. Major tournaments were not as frequent in the early periods as they are today. For instance, the European Handball Championship did not start until 1994. Also, fewer teams qualified for each championship in the early periods. Likewise only four teams qualified for the women's European championship in 1994, compared to 12 in 2017.

approach of the younger generations of Icelandic players – who were bound neither by past defeats and experiences nor by the amateur culture attached to the national teams – helped them establish new ideocultures (see Fine, 2012). This distinct orientation of this younger group to a more professional outlook and the foundation of such an ideoculture made the teams much better equipped than ever before to take on the challenges of facing national teams with more professional background and prestige.

This impact of the younger generation on sport outcomes is evident in many of the successful Icelandic national teams that have emerged. The men's football team was built around a cohort of players born in the early 1990s. They had been successful in the national youth teams and qualified for the European Championship in the Under 21 team – for the first time for Iceland. Finnbogason, a footballer from this generation, says the fact that the national A team qualified for the 2016 European Finals was not a matter of luck:

> Then good players emerged from this core in the u21s. Nine players who are now in the national A team. They really work well together. Good guys; all of them set their standards high. It's not just luck: we are good and we deserve to be playing out there with the 24 best teams in Europe.

He further reflected that shared experience counts in that the players created a shared history of cooperating and coordinating their sporting behavior over a number of years. It took these young players repeated sequences over time to learn and evolve in order to perform well in the A team. They had gone through an elaborate developmental process together as a group and had been brought into the A team at an early age, by the former coach. Gunnleifsson, one of the senior national football players, recognizes the difference in the younger generation, compared to the senior players:

> It all changed in 2012. It was then, when Heimir and Lars took over as coaches of the national team, that they got these 21-year-old lads with incredible individual ambition to achieve success. Bigger egos. They had much better training than we older players had. They were forged into a national team of 21-year-olds and they got good results.

Many players in those teams had been playing together in the Icelandic national youth teams. They knew each other and had experienced the same attitudes towards training and behaving professionally, which were different from those of the previous generation. The younger generation created a new ideoculture that defined their teams by and around the younger players, and the senior players – some of whom had not been behaving professionally within the national teams – even had to adjust to the new emerging culture. This re-definition also occurred in some of the other teams. In the women's handball team, for instance, which qualified for the European finals in 2010, the younger generation changed things for the better. One of the senior players, Anna Úrsúla Guðmundsdóttir, said:

> Some new blood came in with them [the younger players]. They put things in motion and of course they also had this confidence . . . you felt the ambition they had. I think that was a sort of turning point for us.

The tipping points: from "why?" to "why not?"

The "golden age" of Icelandic national sport teams can be traced back to the fall of 2008. Some have suggested that this emergence of Icelandic national teams to the international sports scene is linked with the rebuilding of Icelandic society in the aftermath of the collapse of the Icelandic banks, which resulted in a general economic crash in Iceland in October 2008.[4] Various studies in the literature suggest that collective solidarity strengthens when communities experience external threats, such as in cases of financial crisis, which could have helped the Icelandic national teams get into action (Erikson, 1966; Lauderdale, 1976; Pálmadóttir et al., 2011). It is however both problematic to demonstrate any direct causal relationships between the economic crash and the emergence of national sports success in its aftermath and furthermore not an accurate account of the historical timeline of those events.

Despite the long history of success of the men's handball team, which had lasted over four decades, it didn't win a medal in the top international competitions until August 2008. The Olympic silver became the biggest sporting achievement in the history of Iceland, and it came about six weeks before the financial collapse. Likewise, the women's football team qualified for its first European finals only few weeks after the collapse. Thus, it could be argued that winning the Olympic silver medal not only encouraged the handball team but it also encouraged athletes and teams in other sports in Iceland, and showed them that they could be successful at the international level as well, and this was more important for the Icelandic teams than the motivation from the financial crash. Fine (2012, 48–49) referred to such instances as "triggering effects" which gave the teams confidence in what they could achieve. These events may have intensified some of the important elements of collective spirit and sentiment, which characterize the Icelandic national teams in recent years (see further Chapters 6 and 7). One of the basketball players, Bæringson – who later played a large part in securing access by Iceland's men's basketball team to the 2015 European Finals – acknowledges the importance of such results for other teams:

> I don't know where this confidence came from. Maybe it came from the national handball team, and now the national football team. Maybe we've been infected by them without realising it. I don't want to make comparisons, but I've always been impressed by how they've done things. But if you manage to persuade yourself that those guys are no better than you are, you will simply be better.

Such triggering effects ignited collective feeling and confidence in those teams. These feelings were accompanied by international trends, which saw a narrowing of the gap between the best teams and the rest, providing smaller teams with a better chance of beating the bigger ones. Carsten V. Jensen, a Danish football director, argues:

> The development of sport over the last 20 years has been that everybody can prepare tactically and physically and that's why you can compete, with the best players from Iceland, with almost anybody.

Knowledge on the foundations of skill development such as coaching, nutrition and recovery are more accessible to everyone and that evens the field. Coaches and players who seek such information can easily find it – more easily than 20–30 years ago. This reduction of differences in terms of sports expertise has benefitted smaller nations, and most arguably small and geographically isolated nations such as Iceland.

In recent years all Icelandic teams have started to aim higher. Their coaches – many of them with substantial international experience – led the way by raising the bar in terms of goal-setting, which allowed the Icelandic players to see that they could accomplish something that had not occurred to them before. The men's football coach, Lars Lagerbäck, surprised everyone in his first team meeting when he said that the goal was to qualify for the World Cup or European Finals; at the time, the Icelandic team was ranked by FIFA at No. 133 in the world! One of the senior players recalls the players' reaction: "At our first meeting with the coaches they said the aim was to get us straight into the finals. We laughed at this. No one thought it was realistic." But at the same meeting, Lagerbäck instilled the fundamentals for the team to be successful, as one of the players recalled:

> Lars said at that first meeting that we could beat any team in the world, any team whatever, no matter what it was called, anywhere and at any time. That is, if the preparation was right and each individual gave what he had, one hundred per cent.

One of the junior players in the squad at this time said: "When your coach comes and says, right from the start, that we're going to qualify then you just get down to it and work, and you start believing it when things start going well." Certain matches became tipping points in which the teams started to believe that they had a realistic chance of achieving those high goals. Þráinsson recalls an away game, in which the men's football team was trailing 4–1 against Switzerland and ended up drawing 4–4, as such a tipping point:

> We were trailing by three goals and then we scored our second goal and I could hear that something was about to happen. We ended up drawing the match. All the stadium sensed it. Maybe it was this moment that became the breaking-point for the team. To be able pull such a comeback against such a great football team made us think "we can do everything."

Guðmundur Guðmundsson, the handball coach, was also influential in setting the goal for the national handball team before the Olympics. He recalls: "We set a very clear goal, and set it very high, and not everyone really believed it. But the key men believed it and they worked to have the rest believe in it too." One of the former national team players, Patrekur Jóhannesson, spoke of the importance of setting high goals:

> For the 2008 Olympics, it was as if they were prepared to aim higher. I remember at the time when we were in the national team, all right, we got to fifth place in the World Championships, fourth in the European Cup in 2002 and then fourth in the Olympics, but we didn't really dare aim higher than that.

The bar had been raised and the younger generations were ready for the challenge. They were motivated and hungry for success and felt they had a realistic chance of qualifying for one of the major international tournaments. But it took time for the teams to gain more experience and to learn from their mistakes. The men's football team was close to qualifying for the 2014 World Cup Finals but lost in play-off games against Croatia. But being so close and failing proved to be a major motivation for the team. Many of the players recall the atmosphere in the locker room after the match as a demonstrable shift in the progress towards future directed planning. One of the junior players, Skúlason, described it in these words:

> Actually I think it was good for us not to qualify for the World Cup [in 2014]. We learned an incredible amount from that disappointment. We learned from it and it was so close to us. We decided to do better next time, and that's what we did. We showed, and proved, that we are a good football team, and we showed that we could get through it without going through the play-off games. I think this made us stronger, both as a country and a team.

Losing to Croatia "gave us a sort of sour taste in the mouth and we realised that this was possible at this level," said football player Finnbogason. In addition UEFA decided to increase the number of teams in the European Finals from 20 to 24, which further increased the confidence and motivation of the Icelandic football players to qualify for the next big tournament – which they did.

One of the key elements of the transformation of Iceland's national teams in recent years has been the change in their self-confidence. The "elder-brother complex," which had characterized the Icelandic mentality for decades, had retreated and given place to something more like megalomania. For years, the men's handball team, for instance, lacked the belief that it could beat Sweden, which resulted in the intimidating label *Svíagrýlan* ("the Swedish bogey") in the national discourse. Handball player Stefánsson noted: "There always used to be this obstacle. The obstacle of a population of 300,000. This excuse: we are supposed to be not very good because there are only 300,000 of us." Such hindrances were not only based on an elder-brother complex in Icelandic culture; they were also based on facts. The big nations, such as the Soviet Union in the 1970s and 1980s, were way ahead of others at the time. Stefánsson also noted:

> Maybe there used to be obstacles that we couldn't overcome. We went into competitions and knew we didn't stand a chance in some of the matches. Maybe this was because we always looked at the figures and worked out where we belonged in the rankings and so on. Maybe that wasn't unrealistic back then, but it cast a sort of shadow into later times, when in fact we had normal chances. Then you didn't hear so much talk along these lines.

With time – with good results in international matches and partly inspired by the younger generation – "the elder-brother" psychological barriers were broken, one by one, leading to a more general and collective believe in the Icelandic athletes and teams. This showed in the general discourse of Icelanders in relation to international comparison. The measures of the successes of Icelanders had generally been put forward in the context of *per capita* measurements.[5] Today, however, the phrase "*per capita*" seems to have been left out of the Icelandic vocabulary. "We don't hide behind the '*per capita* excuse' anymore," said sports broadcaster Guðjón Guðmundsson. It has been replaced by stronger self-esteem where athletes began to see the opportunities: "There's a little window, and we are going to throw ourselves through it; then we can win," as Einar Örn Jónsson put it. Icelandic athletes have stopped asking themselves "Why should *we* be able to beat larger nations?" and have starting asking themselves instead: "Why should we *not* be able to beat larger nations?"

Former national coach of the Icelandic ice-hockey team, the Finn Richard Taehtinen, experienced greater belief within the Icelandic players than existed within players from Sweden and Finland. "They think they can beat anyone," says Taehtinen. Sports broadcaster and former handball national player Einar Örn Jónsson sums the whole process up in these words:

> All the other teams won the odd game. Did well here, then badly there. But in the last ten years, I have the impression that all the teams, if we take football, handball and basketball, have adopted this belief that

they can overcome difficult opponents and make it through to a major competition. Which is something that just didn't exist ten or twenty years ago. . . . I am not absolutely sure whether we are actually that much better at all these sports. I think it's more the case that people have got a bit more belief in themselves, their sport and their team. And a bit of a broader outlook. They travel more. There are many more of them, both in football and basketball, and in women's handball and basketball too, who go abroad and play. Maybe this opens their eyes to the fact that there isn't such a great difference as there was thought to be in the old days.

The new outlook in the national teams was characterized by higher levels of ambition, professionalism, optimism, sacrifice and togetherness. The emphasis on aiming higher was evident in the approaches of coaches and players. One of the senior football players, Gunnleifsson, reflects on the changes in the set-up of the national team's games:

> I often relate this anecdote about the way we played in Holland in 2008, and then again last year [2015]. The first time, the meeting started like this: "We're going to play against Holland; this is the team and we're going to try to keep the score to zero as long as we can, and see what happens after that." The second time, the meeting in Holland started like this: "We're going to play against Holland and we're going to beat them."

To sum up, the generation of players which have made up the successful Icelandic national teams in recent years were fortunate to have benefitted from increased professionalism in Icelandic sport, global expertise and opportunities, as well as broader trends in the world of sports. Of course, so have players from the same generation in other nations as well. But this was particularly important for Iceland, being a geographically isolated island with amateur attitudes and methods. Iceland has done extremely well in exploiting the opportunities that have arisen in international sports in recent years, and in building on those successes and transferring them to other teams and to Icelandic sports in general. Thus, it can be argued that for Iceland to break through to the international scene in sport, it was necessary to have younger players who shook things up with their attitude and professionalism. But this by itself was in no way a sufficient element. In the following chapters I will outline how the larger culture and social context in Iceland was crucial for the national team players and teams to reach their full potential in international competitions at the highest level.

Notes

1 See: "Snerist um að djama með strákunum" (article; *Mbl.is.*, 2014, October). See: www.mbl.is/sport/efstadeild/2014/10/17/snerist_um_ad_djamma_med_strakunum/

2 A contrast can be drawn between professionalism and amateurism in this respect. The change from amateur sports towards professional sports represents an ideological shift, transforming relatively unstructured play without specified objectives to a more systematic form of play, resembling conventional work and involving more precise future goals that could be shared among players. This transformation towards professionalism is characterized by an increased emphasis on paid coaches, staff and players; the building of specialized sport facilities; and systematic talent development, which consists of sport specialization, standardized training and the utilization of scientific research from fields such as physiology, nutrition, psychology and business.

3 "The Y generation" refers to those born between 1978–1994 (see Sheahan, 2005)

4 Field notes.

5 "Ísland er besta minnsta land í heimi . . . í fótbolta" (article; *Kjarninn.is.*, 2014, September). See: http://kjarninn.is/greinasafn/island-er-besta-minnsta-land-i-heimi-i-fotbolta/

References

Erikson, K.T. (1966). *Wayward puritans: A study in the sociology of deviance*. New York: John Wiley & Sons, Inc.

Fine, G.H. (2012). *Tiny publics: A theory of group action and culture*. New York: Russell Sage Foundation.

Lauderdale, P. (1976). Deviance and moral boundaries. *American Sociological Review*, 41(4): 660–676.

Pálmadóttir, L.B., Bernburg, J.G., Víkingsdóttir, A.S. and Ólafsdóttir, S. (2011). Fordómar og umburðarlyndi Íslendinga fyrir og eftir hrun. In Á.G. Ásgeirsdóttir, H. Björnsdóttir and H. Ólafs (eds.), *Rannsóknir í Félagsvísindum XII* (pp. 421–427). Reykjavík: Félagsvísindastofnun Háskóla Íslands.

Sheahan, P. (2005). *Generation Y: Thriving and surviving with generation Y at work*. Prahran: Hardie Grant Books.

Shils, E. (1982). *Tradition*. Chicago: The University of Chicago Press.

Swidler, A. (1986). Culture in action: Symbols and strategies. *American Sociological Review*, 51(2): 273–286.

Part III

How Icelanders play sport

6 "The Icelandic madness"

Winning the character contest

> What counts is not necessarily the size of the dog in the fight – it's the size
> of the fight in the dog.
>
> – Mark Twain

National identity

In his book *Art worlds*, Howard Becker ([1982]/2008) argued that all art-
work depends on collective action. Through interaction of people in the
local networks, collective action becomes comprised in local scenes, which
become understood in terms of schools of thought and methods instead
of being related to individual geniuses. Farrell (2001) further argues that
schools of art represent certain styles that are different from those of other
schools of art. The impressionist painters were, for instance, seen as being
different from the Cubists and Surrealists.

The most obvious way to explain the sporting success of nations is to
look at how they play. The style of play is representative of the collective
action and the culture that formed the teams in the first place, stamping them
with a specific identity and characteristics. A former coach of the Argentinian men's football team, César Luis Menotti, spoke of the Argentinian
football identity in the following way:

> Once I heard somebody say that 'there is no national football
> because football is universal.' I would say that man is universal,
> but that the best way to reach universality in any activity is 'to paint
> one's own village.' And Argentinian football players who have left
> the country, from Julio Libonatti to Diego Maradona, became well-
> known because they painted the village with the magic of Argen-
> tinian dribbling, which is bantering, different, with a hallmark of
> identity. I dare to say that I could recognize in any pitch in the entire
> world an Argentinian player.
>
> (Archetti, 1999, 174–175)

For instance, the German steel, Dutch total football and the dribbling Argentinians all represent different schools of how to play the game of football, which becomes a marker of their identity. Icelandic sports also have their own particular characteristics and their styles of play have helped develop an Icelandic national identity in regard to sports. This identity is not based on the belief that the Icelanders possess greater skills or talent in sport than anyone else – on the contrary, they realize that they trail the bigger nations in this respect – but rather the identity stresses the presentation of a strong character in regards to sport.

On the presentation of a strong character, Curry (2008) states that "Action provides opportunities to display character, character being acquired and evidenced when the chips are down. Strong character may be discriminated by such qualities as courage, gameness, integrity, and composure" (107). A strong character can both be displayed by showing mental strength in competition and showing good attitude as a team player. This emphasis on character was a central component of the Icelandic teams whose successes are analyzed in this book.

"The Icelandic madness": the teams in action

In his account of the tradition of Icelandic sports, Stephen Wieting (2015) has described the sports in the sagas as having been played for the sake of honor, both of the individual and of his family and friends. Guðmundur Finnbogason ([1933]/1971, 134–135) has further argued that the history of Iceland shows that Icelanders were not only concerned with winning; it was also important how the contest was won. The Icelanders' identity is based on how others perceive them as victorious. Thus, honor in the context of achieving goals has been important to the Icelanders and still is. Recent cases in Icelandic sport show that athletes want to do well and win and maintain their honor at important competitions – rather like in the Icelandic sagas (Wieting, 2015). What is important is not merely how well you do in the game: it also matters how you play the game.

When the Polish coach, Janus Zerwinsky, took over the Icelandic men's handball team in 1976 he said: "It's interesting to note but you can see that the Icelandic players play with their hearts and souls" (Steinarsson, 1994, 73). Playing with their "hearts" is a shared mentality – a playing attitude – which consists of strong emotional fighting spirit, a belief that anything is possible and a willingness to make sacrifices for the sake of the team. Internationally experienced handball coach Guðmundsson notes:

> I would say that in general, our strengths are hard work, self-sacrifice and a big heart and soul for the game. I think these are very much

Icelandic qualities. These are our strong points, generally speaking. Invincible self-confidence and a desire to win.

"There's a certain charisma, intensity and joy that I think mark us out. I think we are more prepared to show our feelings, feelings of joy, annoyance, anger, more than others are," says Þorgerður Katrín Gunnarsdóttir, former Icelandic minister responsible for sport. In other words, the teams have been identified as playing with their "hearts." Former handball player Jónsson describes the importance of this mindset for Icelandic handballers:

> It doesn't matter if someone has got better technique than you have, or jumps higher or throws harder. If you run just a few more paces than he does, or are prepared to throw yourself in the way of the ball, then at the end of the day you know you will beat him.

Part of the Icelandic athletes' work ethic "lies in our upbringing" argues basketball coach Steinþórsson. Due to the amateur environment of Icelandic sports, young players have to work for what they want to achieve, both on and off the field. Speaking about the character of the Icelandic basketball team at the European championship, Steinþórsson notes:

> They never gave up. That's what we teach them here. When we go on trips for the national team, or to competitions here in Iceland, we have to go collecting bottles and cans [to reclaim the deposits] and we pay almost all the expenses ourselves. While in other countries they get all this pretty well laid on. We have to work for everything. That's how it is in the junior national teams. It's invaluable. We know that's how it is, and this acceptance of hard work is because we know we have to make the effort ourselves. We can't take things for granted.

Others have extended this link between values in the general culture and Icelandic sports ethic, as sports broadcaster and former handball player Jónsson notes:

> By nature we have stamina and perseverance. We are prepared to make everything work: otherwise we couldn't live here. To create a community like we now have here in Iceland has had its cost in every single thing that people do. And it has cost far more effort than is called for in other places to get similar results. To run a symphony orchestra and two professional theatres, for example. These things obviously cost more

here than they do in big cities with populations in the millions. This is a quality that clearly helps us in sports.

In this respect, handball coach Jóhannesson compares the Icelandic players to players in Austria:

> We are hard-working. Both in handball and football, we are prepared to work hard. Just to compare young Austrian and young Icelandic players: here in Iceland I held practices at 6.30 in the morning, and then these kids went on to school afterwards. When I told them this in Austria, they said that would never work out over there.

According to the foreign sport coaches and experts interviewed for this book, a hard-work ethic, a fighting spirit, a belief in oneself, positive teamwork and joy in the game characterize Icelandic athletes and teams rather than sporting talent in and of itself. These attitudes are not sport specific, since they are visible in all the aforementioned teams, but are endemic in Icelandic culture in general.[1]

This character is evident in how the Icelandic teams play. For instance, when the men's handball team competed at the 2008 Olympics, it was faced with major disadvantages in terms of physical aspects in comparison with the other teams (see Figure 6.1) and had to make up for this disadvantage in other terms, most importantly in terms of character.

The other teams had taller, heavier and more experienced players. In the official game statistics of the matches, Iceland did not lead in any aspects of the games, except as regards two-minute suspensions, which was a major disadvantage since the team was a man short on the field of play. But those official statistics only address particular outcomes and technical factors; they do not account for the important and playful team attributes related to the social atmosphere and team morale. With this in mind, I made a content analysis of the games of the men's 2008 Olympic handball team. The analysis indicates that although the team faced many disadvantages in terms of physical attributes and did not lead in important aspects of official game statistics, the players had greater determination than their opponents. For instance, the Icelandic team was more likely to play emotionally in terms of successful game efforts, such as celebrating goals and effective defense play, showing more team support and communication on the field, as well as playing harder than their opponents (see Figure 6.2). The team was in a way what Farrell described as "a delinquent gang," its attitude being different from the established norms in the field of action (2001, 14). In other words, the Icelandic team showed more heart, emotion and fighting spirit on the field than their opponents at the Games (see Halldorsson, unpublished

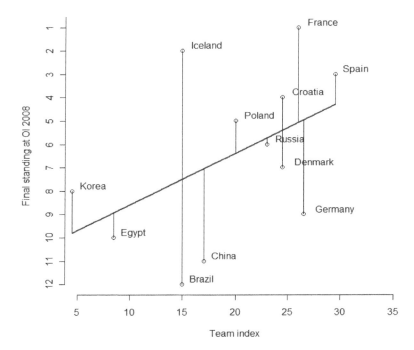

Figure 6.1 Correlations from the men's handball competition at the 2008 Olympics between the team's index (players' height, weight and number of national team games) and their final standing

This figure was made in collaboration with Þórólfur Þórlindsson and Stefán Hrafn Jónsson using data from the Beijing 2008: Handball Official Results Book. Retrieved in 2012 from: www.olympic.org/statistics.

manuscript). This style of play came to be termed as "Íslenska geðveikin" ('the Icelandic madness')[2] and the Icelandic team finished with an historic Olympic silver medal.

According to Fine, "Group products . . . develop through interaction and then may 'catch on,' spreading beyond the boundaries of the originating group and becoming embedded in a national culture" (2012, 38). Thus, "playing with the heart" is today one of the fundamental characteristics of the national team and has become a specific symbol in Icelandic sports, producing the core of "the Icelandic madness." Thus, "the Icelandic madness" has caught on in the other Icelandic national teams as well – apart from the men's handball team – and they even use the same narrative to describe their type of play.[3] All the successful Icelandic national teams have

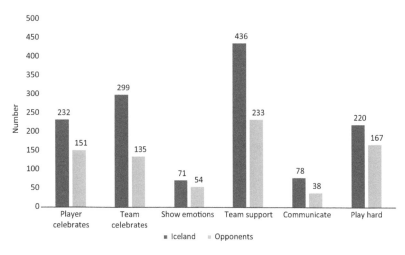

Figure 6.2 Statistics from a content analysis of the social team morale of the Icelandic men's handball team and their opponents from the 2008 Olympics (Halldorsson, unpublished manuscript)

Elite sports increasingly rely on game analyses in the form of statistics. However, most such analyses ignore social elements in team play, such as team spirit and team atmosphere.

these fighting elements in common. Female handball player Guðmundsdóttir describes what "the Icelandic mentality" means to the team:

> It's a bit of a matter of heart that is so valuable for us as Icelanders and for us as a team. The struggle unites us so incredibly much, I think. And our teams too: this tiny hopeless battle all the same. We are this tiny little country and we're always trying to show how good we are. Everyone's working towards the same thing and everyone knows we have to have something extra over and above what bigger nations have. We need this Icelandic madness that is the mark of Icelandic sports. To believe that the impossible can happen.

Thus, "the Icelandic madness" has become a consistent theme – a common identity – within all the national teams. Sports broadcaster Guðmundsson also said:

> What we have is this heart and this madness. You can make an Icelander do the most incredible things, as Bogdan said, if he sees the end goal. But if the Icelander doesn't see the end goal, then it's pointless.

The concept of "the Icelandic madness," which emerged through a collective consciousness shared by Icelandic teams, has become a living thing that breeds players with a common identity, a sense of purpose, feeling of togetherness, uniqueness and confidence. This is evident in the Icelandic basketball team that had shorter players than most of their opponents at the European Championship (see Figure 6.3). "We have to believe more in ourselves than we can really afford to do," says basketball player Bæringsson, whose height is "only" two meters but has been described as playing as if he were much taller. Finnur Stefánsson, one of the national basketball coaches, described this confidence when the national team faces bigger opponents, with a metaphor of the tiny Chihuahua dogs when they encounter larger and physically more intimidating dogs: "We are like Chihuahuas when we face the bigger nations. We stand up to them, challenge them, bark at them and are not afraid to bite them." Accordingly, the men's football team used a photo of a rhino running away from a barking Chihuahua dog, for inspirational purposes, while preparing for their matches in the European finals.

Icelandic sports broadcaster Guðmundur Benediktsson sums up how these attitudes come together and form a collective enthusiasm that is hard

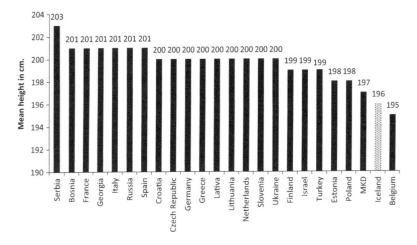

Figure 6.3 Mean height of players of the participating nations in the 2015 Men's European Basketball Championship

Official data from the FIBA website. Available online at: www.eurobasket.2015.org/. In the 2015 FIBA basketball finals, Iceland had the second shortest of the 24 competing teams in the championship. Only Belgium had a shorter team. Iceland also had the smallest number of players under two meters in the competition, three in total, while all their competitors in the group had six or seven players over two meters in height.

to be unaffected by, as he described the atmosphere in the men's football
team during the European Champions finals:

> Just by talking to these guys and being with them, you get filled by a
> sort of exaggerated confidence, this exaggerated confidence that they
> have, and they manage to infect you totally. . . . There's just some feel-
> ing that gets into you as soon as you meet these guys; then you believe
> that we are going to win.[4]

"The Icelandic madness" mentality gets "turned on" when the players are
playing for the national teams. "That fight to the very, very, very end is
something that I have definitely recognized in the Icelandic players," says
the Canadian basketball coach Pederson, and this was echoed by the other
foreign experts. This sort of madness however seems less evident when
playing for club teams. Icelandic basketball player Bæringsson describes
how playing for the national teams magnifies these feelings and sentiments:

> Imagine in an ordinary match that I play here (in Europe), that you came
> up to me at half-time and said: 'If you win this match, you will never play
> basketball again.' (This is just hypothetical, of course.) Then I would
> have to say: 'No, this is my job. I can't sacrifice my whole career for this
> one game.' But the attitude of many of us at the European Cup was that
> if you had said the same thing to us at half-time in those matches, most
> of us would have said OK. We were prepared to sacrifice everything to
> win. We wouldn't have minded losing our little finger or something like
> that. I'm trying to describe how incredibly much those matches mattered
> to us. You just can't compare it with a routine match here in November.

But playing with their hearts and playing emotionally, which has been the
custom in Icelandic sports, is not a sufficient element to do well at the top
level. It is extremely important for a small nation such as Iceland but it has
to be accompanied by discipline, and as has been argued in Chapter 4, the
increased professionalism in Icelandic sports was a critical element in the
success of the Icelandic teams. Emotional play in and of itself can lead to a
loss of direction when players lose focus and do not stick to the organization
of the play. The national football coaches Lagerbäck and Hallgrímsson laid
great emphasis on discipline and a professional attitude within the team.
They wanted players to play with their hearts but to control their emotions.
Footballer Finnbogason reflects:

> Yes, and off the field too: that we were always representing the Ice-
> landic national team. On the field, he [Lars Lagerbäck] didn't want

us to be given any stupid cards. He was very strict about this. I don't remember how many times he reminded us of this in the first games. Both Gylfi and I, and also some others, got some of these stupid cards for arguing with the referee and things like that. He brought this up at every single meeting so we were going crazy about it.

Finally, Becker ([1982]/2008, xv) has argued that a good way to find existing norms is to detect the deviations from the norms. That is, when someone mentions the odd cases, which become the exception that proves the rule. Handball expert Hermundsson said:

> It's been this spirit, this fighting spirit, that has been the mark of the Icelandic team all the time. We don't give up. It's this fighting spirit, which I think is partly that we are part of this nation, this island . . . This is why it was so surprising to see, for example, the women's national team yesterday. Where was this spirit among them? What were they doing? It was really odd to see it, because this has been the hallmark of Icelandic teams, at least to fight, because we don't have the talents. And the same thing, maybe, with our guys in handball at the last tournament: something was wrong.

The Icelandic national teams don't always show this kind of attitude when they play and when they don't, it leaves the spectators surprised, as the quote above illustrates and the history of Icelandic sport shows. But what this analysis proposes is that "the Icelandic madness" is an essential characteristic of the successful Icelandic national sport teams: if they want to do well, they have to play with their hearts.

Winning the character contest

Curry (2008, 107) states that the underdogs have opportunities to display courage when faced with a superior opponent where the showing of good character results in the feeling of pride and maintaining one's reputation whatever the score. This fact shifts the pressure on the team from winning the game to winning "the character contest" (Goffman, 1967, 240). The Icelandic teams are usually in the role of the underdogs and the Icelanders acknowledge that they do not have the most talented players in the world sports pool. They cannot be expected to beat many larger nations; they try, however, to redress this by showing good attitude and character on the field of action – as mentioned above. Athens (1985) argues that such character contests involve not only having nothing to lose, but having something to gain. In return for showing good character, the players receive what

Goffman termed as "moral payments" (1967, 259) from the other team members as well as from the community in the form of being labeled as "strong characters," while those who don't conform to the proposed team character are defined as "weak characters." This focus on showing good character is especially important in such a small society as Iceland, where its players are integrated into the local and national community, where they are bonded in tight networks with their families, friends and neighbors as well as with members of the general public who follow and appreciate national team sports (Athens, 1985). If players show weak character while playing for Iceland, there is no place to hide when they come back home. They will also embarrass their family and friends and find themselves in a situation where "a reputation lost may not be easily regained" (Curry, 2008, 107; see further in Chapter 9).

The framing of sports as winning the character contest sometimes colors the interpretation of who actually won a game, credit not necessarily going to the winning side in terms of the score. The ambiguous criteria of results were noted by Goffman where he stated: "Scoring in some cases may be so flexible that each side can maintain its own view of the final outcome . . . allowing one team to stress score in primary attributes, the other in properties of character" (1967, 247). This is one of the peculiarities of small nations' teams. They adjust to different standards. Thus, small nations, such as Iceland, cannot be expected to beat the bigger nations in sporting contests, but they can win "the character contest" on the field. Footballer Finnbogason says: "The Icelandic attitude is to fight and go for every ball. If you do that, then Iceland will be happy with you." This demonstration of willingness to compete, regardless of the outcome, is what is expected of the Icelandic teams and this is what they try to impress over other teams.

This appreciation of showing good character is evident in regard to the Icelandic national teams. "We felt as if we had won the competition," stated basketball player Stefánsson, after the 2015 European Championship, even though the team lost all its matches. The team focused on all the "small wins" in the game, meaning that they acknowledged and built on task-oriented goals such as blocking a shot, scoring over a big player, hitting a 3-pointer shot, and successfully opening the defense with the team tactics. "We were playing against giants but we were constantly trying to provoke them," says Stefánsson; that was the team mantra: "If we make lots of small wins, we can make the big win." The nation was proud of the character the team showed in the finals. They worked hard, showed good teamwork, never gave up and played with their hearts, which is something that Icelanders greatly value.

This was further evident in the conduct of the Icelandic fans when the men's football team played its first-ever match in the 2016 European finals, against Portugal – who in the end won the championship. Whenever the Icelandic players succeeded at anything on the field the fans cheered, almost as if Iceland had scored a goal. Whether a player won a tackle, the goalkeeper grabbed the ball or when the team won a corner, a loud cheer and applause was heard from the Icelandic fans.[5] The fans were focusing on the "small wins."

Interestingly, the general perception of the results of the 2016 European men's football finals were not perceived in concrete terms, but in abstract terms. When the team lost in the quarter-finals 2–5 against the hosts, France, there was a feeling among the attending fans that "we won" – in part because France had led the game 4–0 at half-time. The Icelandic fans stayed inside the stadium singing and celebrating the achievements and character of the Icelandic team in the competition for up to an hour after the match – while all the French supporters had long since left. This is probably the first football match a team "won" by losing 2–5 in the European championship. The men's handball team likewise "won" the silver at the 2008 Olympics, they did not "lose" the gold. Thus, winning the character contest is something to be expected for the Icelandic teams; everything else is considered a bonus.

How the emphasis on character becomes central to the Icelandic teams

The reputation of the characteristics that have been attributed to Icelandic athletes – that is, as strong characters – affects them and their teams in various ways. First, it gives Icelandic athletes access to, and opportunities to work with, the professional leagues abroad. The foreign sports experts interviewed for this book identified a strong work ethic as an important characteristic shared by Icelandic athletes. The Icelandic players who have been playing professionally abroad have, in this sense, "painted their own village" by showing "good" character and paved the way for other Icelandic players to follow in their footsteps. Archetti has argued that in order to establish a sporting tradition that others might accept, respect and even fear, a nation has consistently to do well in sport (1999, 169). Good work leads to good reputations, which benefit those who follow. Foreign clubs who buy Icelandic players are not trying to buy the best footballers or handballers, says Magnús Agnar Magnússon, a prominent Icelandic sports agent, but they are trying to buy good characters – team players. "They look to South America for skilled footballers, to Africa for physically strong players and to the Nordic countries for good characters," says Magnússon. This shows in that Icelandic players often become team captains in their professional teams abroad.

Second, the favorable characteristics that the current professionals and national team players possess influence other Icelandic players who want to follow their footsteps. Daniel Kahneman (2011, 52–58) has defined this as "priming." That is, when the identity of the Icelandic players is seen as being good characters and hard-working players with a strong fighting spirit, this rubs off onto other Icelandic players in general in the form of social learning through social networks (see Akers et al., 1979; Christakis and Fowler, 2009). Thus, Icelandic players want to retain this identity and this encourages them to behave in this manner. This process of identity retention happens both explicitly, when players are guided, encouraged and reinforced to do the same – as when they are selected for junior national teams on that basis, as Hinriksson notes: "We first and foremost select the right characters for our national teams while foreign scouts are mainly looking at technical skills in the younger players" – as well as tacitly, when players interact with other Icelandic players who possess these attitudes and characteristics (see Polanyi, 1962). Sometimes Icelandic players or coaches are signed for professional clubs after recommendations from other Icelandic players and coaches. "We don't want to let our friends down," says handball coach Jóhannesson, indicating a commitment to keep up the good reputation of Icelandic athletes and their relationships with their friends and acquaintances.

Third, this stereotypical identity of Icelandic athletes as being good characters functions as a "stereotype lift" for Icelandic athletes in general. A stereotypical lift refers to a socio-cultural stereotype that influences performances in positive ways (Shih, Pittinsky and Amabady, 1999). When Icelandic athletes experience their identity positively – as they do in terms of their character in the general discourse – it provides them with the confidence that they possess something special that is important and valued in the professional world of sports and that then becomes the hallmark of the Icelandic national team. "We manage to make our strengths into something challenging for other nations," says basketball player Bæringsson; handball player Gústafsson describes it like this:

> We put more effort into it. This leads to things like 'the Icelandic madness' and so on. . . . it comes out in our will, and the way we turn up for all practices. As you can see in any team you go into: you always think you are the one who is doing the most. It's like that in the national team too: then you are in among 14 or 16 guys who are all prepared to do more than usual. This makes a totality that you can call 'the Icelandic madness' or self-sacrifice or fighting spirit or whatever you want. It's always what results from the extra effort we make. It's been impressed on us over the years that we must do more. If we are not at the top of our game then we can lose to everyone; if we are, then we can beat everyone. The sacrifice involved means that everyone does a bit extra. We are Vikings, and we are fighting.

Fourth, Coakley and Pike define national identity as "feelings of attachment to a nation's history and traditions which create unity and a sense of 'we-ness' among citizens" (2009, 313). Thus, the stereotype lift, which the Icelandic nation gains from being identified as good characters in sport, further gives the nation prestige and contributes towards national pride. The players are often referred to as "Vikings" and they play their part in maintaining this image. The men's football team captain, Aron Einar Gunnarsson, even grew a long beard before the European Finals to emphasize the "Viking" appearance.[6] Archetti (1999) has argued that national sport teams display the virtues and qualities of a nation. He further states in this regard the importance of football for Argentinian society: "Argentina had problems in being identified by others as an important nation. Football made it possible for us to be recognized as something in the world" (1999, 169). Iceland likewise wants to be well presented as a nation. As former minister responsible for sport, Gunnarsdóttir, says: "We want to prove ourselves; we want to show that we matter."

Thus, the narrative of the strong character of Icelandic athletes has created a local tradition of how to play sport, which the junior athletes take as given and try to maintain (see Archetti, 1999; Hobsbawm and Ranger, 1992). This emphasis on the importance of character in Icelandic sports has provided Icelandic athletes and teams with an identity that has proven valuable for the national teams in question. Character has been the key building block in the individual athletes' careers and also in contexts when they join together in the successful national teams.

Notes

1 "Vinnusemi og sjálfsbjargarviðleitni helstu aldamótdyggðir" (article; *Mbl.is.*, 2000, April). See: www.mbl.is/greinasafn/grein/528652/
2 A more appropriate term for this attitude is probably "intensity."
3 See (on football) "Aron Einar: Íslenska geðveikin skóp þennan sigur" (news clip; Fotbolti.net, 2015, June). See: fotbolti.net/printStory.php?id=188918
4 "Gummi Ben: Ég fór út úr líkamanum" (news clip; *Ruv.is*, 2016, June). See: www.ruv.is/frett/gummi-ben-eg-for-ut-ur-likamanum
5 Field notes.
6 See: "Aron um skeggið: Endurspeglar víkinga lookið" (article; *Fotbolti.net.*, 2016, July). See: http://fotbolti.net/news/01-07-2016/aron-um-skeggid-endurspeglar-vikinga-lookid
  This also applies to some of the handball players.

References

Akers, R.L., Krohn, M.D., Lanza-Kaduce, L. and Radosevich, M. (1979). Social learning theory and deviant behavior: A specific test of a general theory. *American Sociological Review*, 44(4); 636–655.
Archetti, E.P. (1999). *Masculinities: Football, polo and the tango in Argentina*. Oxford: Berg.

78   *How Icelanders play sport*

Athens, L. (1985). Character contests and violent criminal conduct: A critique. *The Sociological Quarterly*, 26(3): 419–431.

Becker, H.S. ([1982]/2008). *Art worlds*. Berkeley: University of California Press.

Christakis, N.A. and Fowler, J.A. (2009). *Connected: The surprising power of our social networks and how they shape our lives*. New York: Little, Brown & Company.

Coakley, J. and Pike, E. (2009). *Sports in society: Issues and controversies*. London: McGraw-Hill.

Curry, T. (2008). Where the action is: Visual sociology and sport. *Social Psychology Quarterly*, 71(2): 107–108.

Farrell, M.P. (2001). *Collaborative circles: Friendship dynamics & creative work*. Chicago: The University of Chicago Press.

Fine, G.H. (2012). *Tiny publics: A theory of group action and culture*. New York: Russell Sage Foundation.

Finnbogason, G. ([1933]/1971). *Íslendingar: Nokkur drög að þjóðarlýsingu*. Reykjavík: Almenna Bókafélagið.

Goffman, E. (1967). *Interaction ritual: Essays on face-to-face behavior*. New York: Anchor Books.

Hobsbawm, E. and Ranger, T. (eds.) (1992). *The invention of tradition*. Cambridge: Cambridge University Press.

Kahneman, D. (2011). *Thinking fast and slow*. London: Penguin.

Polanyi, M. (1962). Tacit knowing: Its bearing on some problems of philosophy. *Reviews of Modern Physics*, 34(4): 601–616.

Shih, M., Pittinsky, T.L. and Amabady, N. (1999). Stereotype susceptibility: Identity salience and shifts in quantitative performance. *Psychological Science*, 10(1): 80–83.

Steinarsson, S.Ó. (1994). *Strákarnir okkar: Saga landsliðsins í handknattleik 1950–1993*. Reykjavík: Fróði.

Wieting, S. (2015). *The sociology of hypocrisy: An analysis of sport and religion*. London: Routledge.

7 Teamwork
Playing your own game

Alone we can do so little; together we can do so much.

– Helen Keller

The hero is a convenient way to explain success. This appreciation for heroism has been the case in Iceland where prominent figures such as football coach Lars Lagerbäck and the star and captain of the men's handball team, Ólafur Stefánsson, have been credited as the masterminds of the successes of their teams. But as Robert Putnam has observed, "national myths often exaggerate the role of individual heroes and understate the importance of collective effort" (2000, 24). Thus, the focus on the idolization of key individuals draws attention away from other elements of collective team sporting success. Teams don't do well without effective teamwork.

The national football coach Hallgrímsson points out that Iceland does not have great individual players in football, and former national women's coach Eyjólfsson asks: "Would any member of our team even get into the beginners' teams of our top opponent's? The answer is 'No' in most cases." That is probably the case with most of the Icelandic national teams. They therefore have to base their approach on strong and effective teamwork with the intention of building teams that become greater than the sum of their parts.

Research has shown that successful Icelandic national teams build on strong teamwork (Halldorsson, Thorlindsson and Katovich, 2017). All the Icelandic national teams covered by this study are based on the same cultural ideology. The emphasis on effective teamwork is one of the fundamental prerequisites for the Icelandic national teams. The coaches of all the national teams therefore picked not necessarily the best and most talented players for the national teams, but the right players – that is, the players with the right team attitude. The teams in turn use national motivating symbols and shared meanings for team building, which are often based on nationalism. The players share pasts; they are good friends and feel a responsibility to be "team players."

This emphasis on team play suits Icelandic athletes well. Icelanders tend to do better in team sports than in individual sports, partly because they rely on what has been termed as "open skills," rather than the "closed skills" on which individual sports are based. Closed-skill sports such as swimming and sprinting consist of a solo performance in an unchanging environment and call for individual talent and skill and concentration on finishing the task at hand; open-skill sports (such as football, handball and basketball) occur in a collective, dynamic and changeable environment, and therefore rely less on individual talents and skills and more on situational awareness and interaction (Allard and Burnett, 1985; Poulton, 1957). Icelanders are well suited for open-skill sports. Sports broadcaster Guðmundsson argues, "We are social beings up to a point. This is what has helped us. If we don't enjoy ourselves, then we don't get results."

The team spirit in the successful Icelandic teams has been described as extremely robust by members of all the teams (see also Chapter 6). A 19-year-old basketball player who recently started playing for the Icelandic national youth team stated:

> I have also played for the Swedish national team; there wasn't the same morale there as there is in the Icelandic. It was much more fun playing for Iceland because here everyone plays as one team. We laughed, ate and enjoyed ourselves together. I really like that.[1]

The team members and coaches agree that there are hardly any issues or problems among the players in the teams, or at least nothing that they were not able to solve easily. Accordingly, basketball player Bæringsson describes good teamwork in these terms:

> I think you can define it as meaning that you want to have the others in your team enjoy themselves as much as you are doing. That's how it is in our team, absolutely. There has never been any trouble in this bunch, nothing that I can remember. There's always some trouble in those teams over in Europe. Always something; they aren't happy with their playing times, or their contracts, or something like that. But there's no trouble like that in our national team. People here are in it whole-heartedly. They encourage each other and will do anything for each other. It's a different reality from what I find over there. [*Referring to his experience of playing for professional teams in Europe.*]

Christakis and Fowler argue that people with close connections to one another (few degrees of separation between people) are more likely to act altruistically in social surroundings – which is demonstrated in a lack of selfishness and the desire to help others – than people who are further apart (2009, 298–299). The smallness of Iceland, where people are typically within one degree of separation from other Icelanders (where a person only needs to contact one person he or she knows to get in contact with someone he or she doesn't know) – especially in the same field of action – therefore favors altruistic behavior on the part of their national team members, more so than in larger nations. According to the Dutch football coach Bart Heuvingh, the culture in the Dutch national team is more individualistic: players tend to think about themselves instead of helping their teammates in trouble. "It is an individual-istic culture where everybody blames everybody," argues Heuvingh.

The fact that the players are friends further strengthens their motiva-tions and team bonding. In most cases, they have known each other – or been aware of each other – since childhood. This helps them to connect and come together in the national teams. They create intense shared net-works allowing them to become a band of brothers or sisters. Basketball coach Pedersen says: "That togetherness, that they know each other already, that is something that makes it easier for them to come together. It has not been necessary for us to do that much extra, to build this chemistry." Sports broadcaster Jónsson further argues:

> Everyone comes from the same background, no matter whether you were born in Reykjavík or Húsavík. You all have the same culture and mentality. All the way up through the younger age-groups you are playing against the same guys. You get to know them very early on, and people keep up with each other, right from the beginning. So when you get into the national team, you know all the others. Either you played with them, or you were schoolmates, or you have friends or relatives in common. From the first national team practice, you know them all and have known them already for quite some time. And then further bonds are made in the team.

Although players in national teams other than Iceland's may have played with each other in their youth teams – and formed friendships – this inten-sity of shared histories is not always apparent among those teams accord-ing to the foreign experts. Among Icelandic teams, the shared histories are apparent. Footballer Finnbogason illustrates this point further: "These are all guys I could see myself going on holiday with."

The players in the Icelandic teams do everything they can to play for the national teams: they look forward to the national team sessions where they meet and play with their friends and even "recharge" their batteries after hard seasons in their professional teams. Playing with their friends in the national team is not something they want to miss. "I've never felt, 'No, I can't be bothered.' It's such incredible fun meeting the boys," says footballer Skúlason about playing for the national team. Footballer Vilhjálmsson, who has not recently been selected for the team, even goes so far as to say: "I would fill up the refreshment bottles for the national team if I were asked to do so."[2]

The players join the team events even though they are tired after long seasons with their club teams, and even though they may have some injuries. An example of the sacrifices that Icelandic players make for the nations' teams is when basketball player Jón Arnór Stefánsson – a distinguished professional and one of the best players in Icelandic basketball history – was between contracts at the time when the Icelandic team started to play at the group stage for the European Championship; he therefore had no insurance cover as a professional athlete. He skipped the first group match but after that, he couldn't resist and played all the remaining games in the group without having any insurance. Any injury he may have suffered in any of the games could have ended his career prematurely without any financial compensation to him as a professional athlete. Stefánsson reflects:

> I wasn't in the first match, but it didn't feel right not to be there. I felt bad about it. It was an out-of-character decision, and I thought 'What am I doing?' I was desperate to play and played the rest of the matches. I didn't think too much about it; it was just right for the moment. We had a chance, and there was no real alternative.

His teammate Bæringsson commented on this:

> He [Stefánsson] finished the round without being insured. And that's his work. He's on a good contract for the next two or three years, with a salary. If he just waits for it, and doesn't play. But he decides to throw all that up because he sees this opportunity. This never happens in basketball. If he had been injured he wouldn't have got anything. I need hardly say I've never heard of anything like this anywhere else.

Thus, the motivation for the players in the Icelandic team lies not in earning money or material things – although playing well for the national team can help them to land contracts with professional teams – but rather in the joy of playing sport with their friends and making the nation proud. For the Icelandic national teams much more is at stake than winning or losing: the nation's reputation is at stake. Handball player Gustafsson reflects on how he felt after a disappointing performance by the men's handball team in the 2016 European Championship:

> The first thing you think of when the final whistle is blown is not about yourself and what fun it would have been to have got further. It's more about how people at home in Iceland will be disappointed.

In your own home. With the national team, you put yourself in second place. Perhaps that's the difference between playing for the national team and for clubs over here in Europe. After a lost match over here, you might be annoyed with your own players and you think of things connected with them and how it affects you, and when are we going to going to win a title, and am I starting to lose my grip, things like that. You see these things in completely different terms, all with much more direct bearing on yourself. In the national team there's a different passion at work. You're doing things more for other people rather than for yourself.

This kind of determination and sacrifice is something that is somewhat wanting in professional sports, as can be illustrated in this point from basketball player Stefánsson:

When you play with the national team you play with your heart. You are all in it together and everyone is pleased if any of you does something well; there's no jealousy. It's as if you are taken back in time to when you were at the playground with your friends. There aren't many people in the sporting world today who have this feeling. Where results are measured not so much in terms of money but in terms of pleasure.

The players look forward to meeting their teammates – and friends – in connection with national team projects. Playing for the national team is somewhat different from playing with the professional club teams in this respect. "Coming to play with the guys in the national team recharges my energy," says basketball player Stefánsson; handballer Gústafsson says: "If it wasn't for the national team I wouldn't be playing professionally in some small town in Europe; I would just come home." It is much more fun just playing with your friends in Iceland rather than playing in professional teams. The culture molds the attitude of the participants towards how to play, and this is activated when they are playing with their friends representing Iceland in international competitions.

"Collective individualists": The communal/individual dichotomy

Iceland is a democratic society and much like the other Nordic nations it is characterized by a strong sense of collectivism (Wieting, 2015). This national character helps explain why the Icelandic teams are known for their strong teamwork (Halldorsson, Thorlindsson and Katovich, 2017). Nevertheless, Icelanders have also been noted for strong individualism (see in Gunnlaugsson and Galliher, 2000; Mixa and Vaiman, 2015). This individualistic spirit has especially been noted in business studies, where Iceland has been seen as one of the most individualistic nations in the world (see in Mixa and Vaiman, 2015). But this emphasis on individualism also applies to sport. It is commonly argued that elitists are egoists, and Icelandic athletes are no exception, as the interviews revealed. Former footballer Þráinsson said: "All these guys are egoists and there is competition between them. This is why they do so well. They are great team players none the less. This is something that's hard to explain." The dual character of Icelandic athletes as being simultaneously egoists and team players indicates an interesting dichotomy in the character of the nation. Cerulo (2008) has shown how nations' values are multifaceted and even contradictory.

Aiming for success is valued in Icelandic culture, where people are encouraged to do more than others with this in mind. Through the nation's history the Icelandic people have been noted as hard working (see Finnbogason, [1933]/1971, 163–164). "Hver er sinnar gæfu smiður" ("Each individual creates his own good fortune") runs an Icelandic saying. The encouragement to excel is even built into the youth sport system. Youth sports coaches in Iceland divide participants into groups based on their ability from a young age, and individual prizes are even awarded to 10-year olds who are considered the best among equals. Hermundsson, for instance, says:

> Iceland is different from Norway, where everyone is supposed to be treated equally. Maybe we are more Americanized. It's OK to excel, and to excel early on. That's not popular in Norway, at least not from what I've seen there.

It is considered normal to select the best performers and to aim to be the best performer. The ideology is that everyone should have the appropriate challenges in accordance to their ability. So the best players should train with the best and compete against the best, while those who have lower levels of skill and even less interest in the sport will also compete against their like-minded peers. But these groups are not fixed. Participants can easily move between groups, upwards or downward, which can work as motivation for them to show dedication and commitment in order to move up to a more prestigious group.

Another part of understanding this dual character of communal attitudes and individualism lies in the definition of individualism. Icelandic athletes have not been known for being individualistic in the sense that they believe the needs of each person to be more important than the needs of the group. Basketball player Bæringsson states: "In your club team, what is important to you is how you do as an individual. But I think that whole outlook is put aside when you play in the national team. It doesn't matter who scores." The individual player will make sacrifices for the collective whole. Of the men's football players, the Swedish coach Lars Lagerbäck says: "In terms of character the difference between Iceland and the other Nordic countries is they are a bit more individual. If you want something to happen, you take care of it yourself." Dutch football coach Bart Heuvingh identified the key characteristics of Icelandic athletes as being disciplined team players and that they can generally be described as self-reliant. Icelandic athletes usually take care of themselves and are disciplined in everything they do and in trying to get better; this was the view shared by the foreign experts interviewed for this book. Thus, independence is probably a more valid description of this kind of behavior than individualism.

The element of independence is further evident in how the Icelandic players conduct themselves in the teams, manifesting itself as active participation and individual agency rather than passive participation. The Icelandic teams are based on what can be described as an "organic solidarity" in the Durkheimian sense of the word (see Halldorsson, Thorlindsson and Katovich, 2017). This emphasis on organic solidarity means that the players contribute to team development – opposed to a "mechanical solidarity" in which the coach is in sole charge and the players simply follow instructions from the coach. All the Icelandic national teams' coaches seek and value the input of their players. This process of seeking is more evident is some teams than others and the players in some teams make more use of this than in others. The men's handball team has particularly been known for the collective agency within the team where the players are active in the decision-making process (Halldorsson, Thorlindsson and Katovich, 2017; Thorlindsson and Halldorsson, 2017). In the team's time-outs, for instance, the players often take charge and make decisions on how to play while the coach takes a step back. This is evident in the most successful Icelandic handball teams that depend more on such individual agency than do their opponents' teams (Halldorsson, unpublished manuscript). This was also the case with the successful and legendary Swedish handball team in the 1990s. Input from the players is crucial, according to handball coach Guðmundsson:

This is an absolutely crucial point in my opinion. If it's a case of the coach and the players, or me and them, that probably won't get results. It has to be a joint project. Otherwise it's easy to blame someone else if things don't work out. This is an incredibly important part of building a team up.

Basketball coach Pederson says:

Sometimes the players in the game situation have a better feel for some things than the coach standing on the outside. They are right in the middle of the action. If they have a suggestion within the game . . . I'm all open for it.

Football coach Lagerbäck says that the coach has very little influence on the team after the match starts. There is no use shouting something from the sidelines since the players can't hear the coach. So the coach has to rely on how they will respond to the play on the pitch, without getting directions from the coach. In other words, the athletes are encouraged to show initiative on and off the field. In this context the independent nature of Icelandic athletes – manifested in individual agency – contributes to the building of effective teamwork, fostering team spirit, strengthening players' commitment, self-efficacy and responsibility and helps players respond to the dynamic action on the playing field (Halldorsson, Thorlindsson and Katovich, 2017).

Thus, the national teams successfully combine the elements of individualism and collectivism in the sense that players are ambitious and work hard to try to improve, and strive to make the most of their opportunities, and they also respect their teammates and are willing to fight for each other. This dual attitude is epitomized in the star men's football player, Gylfi Sigurðsson. He has played in the English Premier League and in the German Bundesliga and is undoubtedly the most talented Icelandic football player of his generation and the key player of the current historic national team. He would not have reached this stage without being an egoist in this sense. He has relentlessly pursued his football career with deliberate practice from a young age and by promoting himself abroad. As the star player of the Icelandic team, he could undoubtedly demand a role on the field that would give free range to his skills – where he could have a role as "the football ten" in the team's formation (a role most players dream of) – but he doesn't. He runs, fights and does all these unnoticeable – but important – pieces of "dirty work" for the national team. He leads by example. Sigurðsson's unselfish efforts on the field also motivate other players to do the same, as these comments by his teammate Skúlason describe:

> We've got the best man in our team. He plays in the biggest team of us all, in the English Premier League. He's such a good fighter. He wants to win, and to score and to get the ball,' and so on. But he wants to work for the team. You don't see the best players in the bigger teams doing that.

Various values may prove their worth in circumstances where they confer advantages (Goffman, 1967). According to Cerulo (2008) certain values take over under special circumstances. "Communalistic relations" are one type of social relation that are applicable with the Icelandic teams:

> [They] refer to a context in which social actors become connected via a specific task, event or characteristic . . . a sense of familiarity, "like-mindedness" or "we-ness" emerges and the good of the community takes precedence over any subgroup or individual. Similarities are stressed over differences and common knowledge is stressed over specialized knowledge.
>
> (Cerulo, 2008, 357)

Icelandic athletes may be driven by individualistic values and motivations in environments where those values are prevailing – such as in the professional clubs where they approach their sport as work – and by more communal values and motivations in other environments, such as the Icelandic national teams where their sport is experienced more as play with friends and as a means of making their nation proud rather than as work (see further in Chapter 8).

The importance of playing your own game

Finally, one of the characteristics of how the national teams play is that they draw on their strengths. One of the major disadvantages of Iceland's being a small nation is that it is difficult to combine a number of players with enough talent or the "right" physical attributes for the national team at the same time: there is a limited pool of players to choose from and the outcome may be that teams lack ideal team attributes. This lack of physical resources usually leaves the Icelandic teams in the role of the underdogs.

While many of the larger nations have developed a playing strategy for their national team – which is taught through all the junior teams in order to make the juniors ready to play "the right way" when they reach the senior team – and in which the right players are brought into the system, smaller nations such as Iceland have to use other methods. They do not have the luxury of having a catalogue of players from which to select the right player for the particular team strategy. They have to constantly evaluate and think about the right way to play, depending on which players are available for the national team at any given time. Handballer Stefánsson reflects: "Now, for example, the new national team coach will have to give this careful thought. He'll have to choose on the basis of character and physical capacity and base his system on that." This option is one of the things that set the Icelandic teams apart from those of many of the larger nations. It has forced the Icelandic teams to use all their player resources thoroughly, while the larger nations can just drop players who do not fit in the system, make mistakes or do not function as part of the team and bring in others with the right attributes instead. In other words, the Icelandic teams have to stick to the players they have and play on their strengths.

Drawing on particular strengths rests on building the strategy that best suits the players in the team at any given time. The men's football team faced some criticism for how it played at the European Championship finals in 2016. Its way of playing, which consists of organized, tactical and defensive football, long balls and emphasis on set-plays – which results in low percentage of ball possession – has been labeled by some as "negative" football.[3] Football coach Hallgrímsson emphasized the importance for Iceland of playing that way – instead of some other way: "I've often said that if we set out to play like Spain, then we would be a lousy imitation of Spain and would never achieve anything." Sports broadcaster Jónsson argues:

> There's really only one way for us to do anything as a team, and that is to make up the best team we can from the people we've got available. And then the best game style for the players you have. Rather than say: 'We are going to play this sort of game, or that sort of game,' and then start trying to change your players to suit. I don't think that would ever work for us.

Football coach Eyjólfsson based his approach to the women's football team on this strategy:

> Everyone wants to play Barcelona-style football, but you have to have the players for it. . . . We build our tactics around the strengths of our players. Because our team wasn't good at keeping the ball, you had very limited time for improving their passing technique. So you have to work on a particular tactic for your team that won't expose its weaknesses.

The coaches of the men's football team found the right strategy with the right mix of players to get maximum results. This combination of strengths can be seen from the fact that in the European Finals the Icelandic team fielded the same starting 11 players in all its five games in the tournament; these were the right players for the most efficient strategy for the Icelandic team in the European Championship adventure. The Icelandic teams had to use their limited resources to the full extent.

The Icelandic teams have also had to find some new ways of doing things that will give them some kind of edge over their opponents. The basketball and handball teams have been noted for playing an unorthodox game. The

German NBA star Dirk Nowitzki described the playing style of the Icelandic basketball team as follows: "They have an unorthodox style, they have a lot of smalls, they got a lot of shooters, they're crafty, they've got some fighters in there . . . they're warriors and deserve all the credit."[4] The famous proverb "Necessity is the mother of invention" applies to the Icelandic teams in this context. Since they are disadvantaged in many aspects of the game, they have to find new ways of doing things. They are forced to adjust to their underdog role – in terms of players' height and weight on the field – with new methods and solutions. Basketball coach Pedersen explained the unorthodox strategy of the basketball team:

> We don't play with a typical center who plays and scores most of their points close to the hoop. We did not have that luxury of having a player of that high quality. So some of the things we did offensively were very unorthodox. We were setting big screens for the big players instead of the other way around. The other teams play the same style, and we were pretty much just the opposite of that. . . . We kind of changed our problem of lack of height and tried to make it a problem for the other team. Make some of their biggest players play defense in a way they are not used to.

Likewise, because of their lack of height, the handball team had to invent a new way of playing defense in the middle of the 2008 Olympic Games. The coach, Guðmundsson, describes it in these words:

> We developed a certain defensive strategy that suited us. At the start we intended to play a completely different type of defense, but I saw it wouldn't work and dropped it. . . . It grew up from the players we have . . . I realised, as their coach, that we wouldn't beat them [Poland in the quarter-finals] by doing something traditional. Of course the players were very much involved in this, in giving it shape. And we did it in a very short time. We had one 50-minute practice session to try it out. It is very unusual. The defense was extreme, and unorthodox. We changed all the rules, more or less. It was quite an achievement, a completely revolutionary defense. The national team has been playing this more or less all the time since 2008.

The innovative defense that Iceland played in the 2008 Olympics broke the key rules of the Swedish legendary 6.0 defense which had gained hegemony in international handball since the early 1990s. This defense was also based on surprising the opponents by changing the defense system in mid-play (playing a 3.2.1 or 3.3 system) when the attacking team was set to execute its offensive strategy. This fresh and innovative way of playing defense has since been picked up by many teams in international handball. The collective agency and emotional play of the handball team facilitated the creative process within the team (see Parker and Hackett, 2012), which gave it an advantage over its opponents and led to the winning of the Olympic silver medal.

Thus, the Icelandic teams, due to the low population of Iceland and the absence of world-class players, have to build their approach on strong teamwork and friendships, playing from their strengths and to try to find new and unorthodox ways of playing – making their strengths a problem for the opposite teams.

Notes

1 "Miklu skemmtilegra að spila fyrir Ísland" (article; *Mbl.is.*, 2016, November). See: www.mbl.is/sport/korfubolti/2016/11/24/miklu_skemmtilegra_ad_spila_fyrir_island/
2 "Matthías: Ég myndi fylla á brúsana fyrir landsliðið ef ég væri beðinn um það" (article; *Visir.is.*, 2016, November). See: www.visir.is/matthias – eg-myndi-fylla-a-brusana-fyrir-landslidid-ef-eg-vaeri-bedinn-um-thad/article/2016161109032
3 "Joachm Löw ekki ánægður með leikstíl liða eins og Íslands" (article; *Visir.is.*, 2016, June). See: www.visir.is/joachim-low-ekki-anaegdur-med-leikstil-lida-eins-og-islands/article/2016160618919
4 A quote from the post-match television interview of Germany versus Iceland at the 2015 European Championship. See further here: "Germany win European Basketball opener" (article; *Dw.com.*, 2015, September). See: www.dw.com/en/germany-win-european-basketball-championship-opener/a-18695965

References

Allard, F. and Burnett, N. (1985). Skill in sport. *Canadian Journal of Psychology*, 39(2): 294–312.
Cerulo, K. (2008). Social relations, core values, and the polyphony of the American experience. *Sociological Forum*, 23(2): 351–362.
Christakis, N.A. and Fowler, J.A. (2009). *Connected: The surprising power of our social networks and how they shape our lives*. New York: Little, Brown & Company.
Finnbogason, G. ([1933]/1971). *Íslendingar: Nokkur drög að þjóðarlýsingu*. Reykjavík: Almenna Bókafélagið.
Goffman, E. (1967). *Interaction ritual: Essays on face-to-face behavior*. New York: Anchor Books.
Gunnlaugsson, H. and Galliher, J.F. (2000). *Wayward Icelanders: Punishment, boundary maintenance, and the creation of crime*. Madison, WI: The University of Wisconsin Press.
Halldorsson, V. (unpublished manuscript). "Að spila með hjartanu:" Innihaldsgreining á leikjum íslenska karlalandsliðsins í handknattleik.

Halldorsson, V., Thorlindsson, T. and Katovich, M.A. (2017). Teamwork in sport: A sociological analysis. *Sport in Society*. Available online at: http://dx.doi.org/10. 1080/17430437.2017.1284798.

Hofstede, G., Hofsted, G.J. and Minkov, M. (2010). *Cultures and organizations, software of the mind: Intercultural cooperation and its importance for survival.* New York: McGraw-Hill.

Mixa, M.W. and Vaiman, V. (2015). Individualistic Vikings: Culture, economics and Iceland. *Icelandic Review of Politics and Administration*, 11(2): 355–374.

Parker, J.N. and Hackett, E.J. (2012). Hot spots and hot moments in scientific collaborations and social movements. *American Sociological Review*, 77(1): 21–44.

Poulton, E.C. (1957). On prediction in skilled movements. *Psychological Bulletin*, 54: 467–478.

Putnam, R. (2000). *Bowling alone: The collapse and revival of American community.* New York: Simon & Schuster.

Thorlindsson, T. and Halldorsson, V. (2017). The cultural production of a successful sport tradition: A case study of Icelandic handball. *Studies in Symbolic Interaction* (in press).

Wieting, S. (2015). *The sociology of hypocrisy: An analysis of sport and religion.* London: Routledge.

Part IV

How culture affects sport

8   The value of play

When you enjoy what you do, work becomes play.

– Martin Yan

The professionalization of sport[1]

In the twentieth and twenty-first centuries, sports have moved away from the ideals of the amateur athlete and have become increasingly standardized and professionalized, more so than ever before (Collins, 2013; Guttmann, 2004). With advances in technology and the science of sports, sports performance has improved substantially. Increased mass interest and the globalization of sport have led to the further commercialization and glorification of modern sports. In such sports, winning is considered everything and to maximize the likelihood of winning, a systematic approach to the organization and playing of sport is required. Globalization has brought increased homogenization, standardization, and uniformity to sports across national boundaries (Collins, 2013; Jarvie, 2003). It is in this context that sports have not only become professional, but also mechanical.

The philosophy of professionalism is often driven by extrinsic motivational factors, where the end product is the only goal that matters. This systematic way of practicing and playing professional sport is in sharp contrast to the perspective of sport as play (Collins, 2013). Modern professional sport has become more like work, which consists of achieving maximum effectiveness, which requires calculated, monotonous and specialized actions. The spontaneous, creative and enjoyable nature of sport viewed as play has been minimized in professional sport. These trends led Beamish and Ritchie to argue that while there are notable differences in national sport systems today, they all share common essential characteristics, which are based on the notion of sport as work:

> World-class sports today include the systematic use of pure and applied scientific research to enhance physical performance; the early

identification, streaming and specialization of athlete talent; professional coaching, the use of professional nutritionists, biomechanicians, exercise physiologists, and sport psychologists; carefully organized training facilities with state of the art equipment and instructional technologies; and financial reward systems and incentives for athletes and sport associations.

(2006, 138)

Some have referred to such aspects of professional sports as the "dehumanization" of sport (Billing, Franzén and Peterson, 2004), and interestingly those "common and essential characteristics" do not seem to apply very well to describe Icelandic sports (as we have seen in the former chapters). In Iceland there are furthermore no hi-tech laboratories, in which athletes go through various tests in order to achieve maximum efficiency and results; no systematic doping schemes to gain physical advantage; no hidden technological innovations to give teams an advantage in how they train or play; hardly any systematic talent identification programs, where children around the country are selected for specific sports; no genetic searches for favorable physiological traits, where potentially talented individuals and their parents are tested and measured in order to develop the ideal future elite athletes and there is little emphasis on sport specialization in early childhood aimed at mastery of one sport. All of these have been implemented in many nations that have excelled in sports (Beamish and Ritchie, 2006; Bloomfield, 2003; Epstein, 2013; Hill, 2007; Shogan, 1999). The case of the Icelandic teams creates an interesting contrast with the professionalized reality witnessed in elite sports; they emphasize the importance of sport as play rather than as work and the importance of showing good character rather than an instrumental win-at-all costs philosophy.

Sport as competitive play

After Iceland defeated England in the pre-quarter-finals at the men's football European Championship in 2016, a Welshman described his feelings while watching the game as follows:

> England supporters: please don't be offended by this post; it's not meant to be disrespectful either of you or your team – far from it – but here was me (= Welsh) in Italy, in a bar, watching the match with about fifty Italian blokes, all yelling our heads off for Iceland. It wasn't anti-English, it was pro-Iceland. Pride, passion, commitment, teamwork, playing to their strengths, playing for one another and for their people, god alone knows what percentage of the Icelandic population in the stadium cheering them on: it just reminded us for a few extraordinary

moments of when football belonged to *us*; when it was *our* game, not some multi-national product at the beck and call of big business and geared to their requirements, not ours. Remember when football felt like that? When we were kids, and every game was the World Cup Final and you'd just scored the winner? Well just for a moment, in a bar, that was us: fifty Italian blokes and a Welsh guy all yelling our heads off for a tiny country's team which had just reminded us of what football used to feel like. And they won.[2]

It has long been noted that Icelanders approach their tasks as competitive play (Finnbogason, [1933]/1971; Halldorsson, Thorlindsson and Katovich, 2014). Those emphases can be traced all the way back to the Vikings in the Icelandic sagas. The Vikings used to compete in various contests related to strength and honor (Wieting, 2015, 72–82). Competition and play as elements in day-to-day occupations can also be seen in Iceland's fisheries. Trawling crews who went to sea in the late twentieth century did so in competition with other trawlers, with the day's catches announced in the same way as football scores are today (see Thorlindsson, 1994). This competition of play and desire to compete also applies to sports. Philosopher Sigurður Nordal reflected on the amateur, but competitive, ethos which characterized the late twentieth century Iceland in the following way:

It becomes the duty of the experienced men to impress on others that physical exercise and sport confer their own benefits that are more valuable than any external elements . . . It is beautiful that the amateur ethos does not allow athletes to exploit their sport. If they don't do what they are supposed to do for the sake of the sport itself, then it's better that they should do it from motives of competitiveness and ambition rather than being bought or coerced to do it.

(1987, 301)

Icelanders used to play for the sport itself, not for money, stated Finnbogason ([1933]/1971, 134–135). A foreign expert, Rini de Groot, has argued that the Icelandic teams still retain some of that purity of motivation. "I am convinced of this," he said, contrasting the situation in the Netherlands where elite athletes are more driven by money and fame. Former footballer Þráinsson agrees: "We have this purity. And the players are thinking about the national teams. No matter how high their salaries, they have this huge ambition for Iceland."

Studies of Icelandic elite athletes have shown that they are intrinsically motivated (Halldorsson, Helgason and Thorlindsson, 2012). "For me football has always been a hobby first and foremost. But not only something to have fun from. It's also something to work at and to give vent to my feelings," says female footballer Viðarsdóttir. In this connection, several sociologists have identified a craftsmanship approach as fruitful for successfully completing a task in various fields of action (Harper, 1987; Mills, [1951]/2002; Sennett, 2008; Thorlindsson, 1994; Veblen, [1914]/2006). Craftsmanship emphasizes, for instance, holistic understanding, experimentation, intrinsic motivation and a task-oriented approach, opposed to a more formal authoritarian, mechanical and goal-oriented approach. Many of the craftsmanship elements are evident in how Icelanders play sport.

These intrinsic and amateur values are instilled in youth sports in Iceland. Participation rates are high and the main reason why children in Iceland play sport is that it is fun (Íþróttabandalag Reykjavíkur, 2009). Footballer Viðarsdóttir further notes:

> I never wondered whether, by playing with boys, I was aiming at becoming a professional. For me it was more of a game, I played more just "for the love of the game." Football is what I enjoyed most. That was my play, instead of playing with dolls or playing computer games. It was my way of playing and the way I let off steam.

The organization of sports in the sports clubs is formal in the sense that they have provided formal coaches and often follow a formal curriculum. However, it can also be defined as informal, as games in the clubs tend to resemble playground games. Youth football coach Hinriksson recalls an analysis by a Norwegian specialist who had watched practice sessions in youth football clubs in all the Nordic countries. He came to the conclusion that while the training in Norway, Denmark and Sweden was more formal and structured, where players were taught "the right way" to play, training in Iceland and Finland was more informal, where players were learning in a more innovative way. The Icelandic coaches organize practices, select sides to play and then drink coffee and even make a telephone call while watching the game. They interfere when somebody gets hurt but more or less let the games take care of themselves. Former PE teacher Anton Bjarnason goes so far as to say: "What I think is missing from training of children and teenagers here is that there is so little teaching." "It's like street-football within formal settings," said Hinriksson. He further uses this technique in his coaching:

> I use this a lot with the teams I coach. "If I were to tell you all the answers then you would only be as good a footballer as I am. You have to make the decision. It must be your decision." They have to have freedom within the game, and I think that helps them a lot.

Another aspect of the emphasis on play in Icelandic sports is that despite playing professionally – in various leagues around the world – the national team players however still don't get paid for playing for the national teams. They only recently started receiving *per diem* allowances to cover expenses on national team trips, but nothing else. This applies to all the teams except the men's football team which, again only recently, has begun to receive some financial rewards. All the other teams can still be defined as total amateur teams in this respect. Sports broadcaster Guðmundsson reflects on the issue in these words:

> The amazing thing is that these are professional athletes. Many of them have been on good salaries for years and years with their club teams. Yet they are still making these sacrifices, playing in their spare time for the national team. Without getting anything for it, besides maybe injuries. And they go on doing it. That's heart.

Former handball player Jóhannesson says: "We have all lost, financially, by going in for the national team, but I mean, that was never an issue." This applies to most of the national team athletes. But nevertheless they almost always show up for the national team's engagements. Basketball player Bæringsson argues that this is an important element in the Icelandic teams: "the driving force behind all this is amateurism. No one is tempting us with money to make us play in the national team. It's more the closeness between us."

Scholars have noted that the increased idolization and commercialization of modern athletes is having a rather deleterious effect on sports (Corte, 2013; Eitzen, 2016). But when the Icelandic athletes play for their national team they still hold on to those elements of playing with friends and playing for the sake of playing. The coach of the Finnish men's football team summed it up in this way when asked about the difference between the Icelandic players playing for the national teams and players of other teams: "They take the 'club chip' out and put their 'national team chip' in, and that's the difference."[3]

Professionalism and amateurism: how Iceland is gaining the best of both worlds

As part of this study I visited several professional football clubs in different countries. During one of these visits, in Holland, I was picked up by a Dutch, Turkish-born taxi driver in his forties. He was a keen football fan and had watched all the games of the Dutch and Turkish teams in the preliminary rounds of the men's European Football Championship, which included their games against Iceland. He summed up the difference between the three teams in these words:

> The problem with the Turkish national team is that they play with their hearts and not with their heads; the problem with the Dutch team is that they play with their heads and not with their hearts; but the Icelandic national team plays both with their heads and with their hearts.[4]

This narrative illustrates how the two opposing ideologies of modern sports, amateurism ("the hearts") and professionalism ("the heads"), are merged and crystallized in how the Icelandic teams play.

Icelandic sports have been built around amateurism (see the previous chapters). They are played for fun and are to be played fairly. In Iceland it has not been the "win-at-all-costs" ideology that has counted, but rather a commitment to playing for the sake of playing. When the first foreign handball coach, Janus Zerwinsky, came to Iceland in 1976, he noted that the players only wanted to play attack, they wanted to shoot and try to score, with little or no emphasis on disciplined play or playing defense (Steinarsson, 1994). Likewise, when the men's football team played Denmark in 1967, the team played all-out-attack football, with little discipline and no emphasis on playing defense. Anton Bjarnason, who played in that notorious game, remembers: "The positioning was absolutely hopeless. We had five players playing almost as strikers, who never came back again behind the half-way line." The Icelandic players wanted to score goals, much like in street-football. It also mattered that this was the first game of the team that was shown live on television and the Icelanders did not want to be judged by playing defensive and "negative" football. Denmark won 14–2! The national teams of today have evolved from this local sports tradition. These two examples illustrate the playful nature and the amateurism of how sports have been played in Iceland. This is further evident in how Icelanders approach and organize sports. The secretary-general of the Icelandic Youth Association, Þorsteinsdóttir, notes that the Icelandic attitude is characterized by a sense of hasty initiative and even carelessness. "Þetta reddast" ("It'll be OK") is a common Icelandic phrase, used to cover eventualities where no real planning is done and people just rush into something and see how it goes. This was the approach in the female gymnastics team, according to Þorsteinsdottir:

> It's this Icelandic attitude: it'll be OK. Many other people would never embark on a thing in this way. There's no foundation. But we just go into it, somehow it'll be OK and work out in the end. No one would go ahead with something like this on the basis of what there is on paper.

However, as noted before (see Chapter 4), Icelandic sports have, in recent decades, been strongly influenced by global expertise which has contributed towards growing professionalism in Icelandic sports in general. The effects of this specific foreign sport expertise renovated the Icelandic teams, and took them to the next level, which resulted in their qualifying for major international championships. Without this professional expertise, the teams would not have advanced in important areas which were necessary for qualifying for top-level tournaments. Handball was the first of the Icelandic team sports to gain advantage from these trends and the first sport in which Iceland scored international success. These influences were felt later in basketball and football. With the influx of global expertise, sports in Iceland have progressed in all areas (see Chapter 4). Through the effects of globalization, Icelandic sports have, in recent years, become more organized, structured and professional. The global trends have been transmitted to Iceland through various channels and helped Iceland to build a sports infrastructure that, on top on the emphasis on playing with friends, has helped it to produce successful national teams.

Tomas Peterson (2008) has described Scandinavian sports as consisting of a mixture of amateurism and professionalism:

> The success of the Scandinavian sports model builds on a reasonable balance between two tasks, which exist simultaneously and stand in an ambivalent relation to each other: democratic fostering and competitive fostering.
>
> (6)

This description applies to Iceland as well. Thus, influences from professional global expertise have blended together with local traditions in Icelandic sports. The Icelandic national teams build, on the one hand, on professional attributes such as more work-like training, solid organization and systematic teamwork, and on the other on local values, such as intrinsic motivation, joy of the game and to approach sport as play. In other words, due to the resiliency of Icelandic amateurism against the domination of professionalism, the blending of global expertise with the local Icelandic sports culture has made Icelandic sports become more professional, but not too professional, thus building a well-balanced base which has been important for the recent successes of Icelandic national teams.

The foreign coaches were experts in the field of their sport and brought important sports "know-how" to Icelandic sports. However, they were not impeccable and sometimes lacked the social skills that the Icelandic players were used to. Icelandic athletes wanted to have fun and play with their friends, which was a foreign concept to many of those coaches. The coaches came from another tradition and culture and the blending of different cultural styles was not always smooth. Thus, the Icelanders had to sort out what they needed and what was appropriate in the Icelandic context, and leave other things out. "Bogdan [Kowalczyk] taught us how to do things, and how not to do things," recalls one of the Polish handball coach's former players who later himself became a national handball coach, and who was critical of some of his methods.[5] This view is still evident in Icelandic sports today. East European coaches who coach youth gymnastics in Iceland, for instance, are sometimes criticized for making sport like work rather than play. Such an approach does not go down well with the parents of Icelandic children who practice sport and the foreign coaches have had to adjust to the cultural way sport is perceived and practiced in Iceland.

Collins (2013, 31) has argued that the concept of amateur sports was rooted in the nineteenth-century ideas of sportsmen behaving like gentlemen and of sport being played fairly. This view of sport as play, which is to be engaged in a gentlemanly manner, is still something that can be seen within the Icelandic teams. Ragnar Sigurðsson, a player in the men's football team, has criticized unsportsmanly behavior in football, such as when teams try to pass the time at the end of games with the intention to "kill" games.[6] Accordingly, the Swedish football coach Lagerbäck brought more professionalism to Icelandic football in terms of discipline and professional know-how, but he also acknowledged the general amateur and innocent approach of the Icelandic athletes. However, he urged the team to become more professional, as this example from a post-match interview after Iceland conceded a late equalizer against Hungary at the 2016 European Championship finals illustrates:

All the same I respect our players; with them there's no cheating or nonsense. They don't stoop to any dirty business such as diving; they demonstrate a healthy attitude and treat everyone with respect. But they need to know how to kill time in games, for example when we are going to take a long throw-ins. Then we have to wait for ten seconds and be a bit more detached.[7]

Icelanders have also shown resistance to some of the professional methods used to win. While the national teams are predominantly built around Icelandic players – with only a few exceptions in the history of Icelandic handball – there are strong incentives to buy players from other countries to play for the national teams. "This is what the other nations do," said basketball coach Finnur Stefánsson, who was approached at the European Championship by foreigners who advised him to buy some tall foreign players – which the team desperately needs – from other nations to play for the

Icelandic team. The Icelandic coaches were not interested "because it would take the 'heart' out of the team," said Stefánsson.

The blending of the two opposite ideologies and methods has been favorable and it can be argued that Icelandic sports have in recent years gained the best of both worlds. In this context it often appears that it takes major societal trends twenty years to travel from the Nordic countries over the North Atlantic to reach Iceland. Icelandic sports today are in many aspects similar to those of the Nordic countries in the 1980s and 1990s (see Andersen and Ronglan, 2012). Around 20 to 30 years ago, Scandinavian sports were amateur sports, experiencing the beginning of the professionalization process. This experience came to change the foundations of sports in those countries, resulting in the situation we know today. The men's Nordic football league, for instance, became more professionalized in the 1980s. This professionalization led to instant progress and some of the peaks of the national teams' achievements – particularly in men's football in the 1990s. But this success was followed by further implementation of professionalism in those countries – with various consequences – and the national teams' achievements started to decline. For instance, the Norwegian football success in the 1990s, which resulted in the team's only three qualifications for major tournaments, proved to be short-lived and had disappeared only a few years later: the men's team has not qualified for a major championship since 2000.

There are many similarities between the cases of Norwegian football in the 1990s and Iceland's in the 2010s.[8] In recent years, Iceland has been in the right place at the right time in the historical development of sport, just as Norway was, in football, two decades earlier. Today, there are similar tendencies to professionalize sports in various ways in Iceland, just as there were in Norway at that time. But increased professionalization, with all its benefits, could also present some dangers to how Icelanders play and approach sport, and the achievements of its national teams. If Iceland should draw any lessons from the cases of other Nordic nations then the most important thing would be to recognize and acknowledge the key strengths of Icelandic sports, which made the recent successes possible, and how they differ from the characteristics of sports in other nations where professional sports are more established, particularly in those that are considered to be underperforming in the international arena.

This mixture of professionalism and amateurism – which currently is the state of Icelandic sports – makes an ideal context for excellence: the organized and systematic approach from the professional world of sport blending with the informal play-like approach of the local amateur scenes in Iceland, resulting in teams that play with both their "hearts" and their "heads." Other studies have also stated that some kind of mixture of work and play is important in this respect (Bale, 2007; Shogan, 1999). But whether this state of affairs will hold for Iceland, with increased emphasis on professionalization of sports, remains to be seen.

Notes

1 Parts of this text, on the professionalization of sport, was co-written by Þórólfur Þórlindsson.
2 A response to the article "Iceland's toppling of England at Euro 2016 is a triumph for the little guys" (a reader's response; *Theguardian.com.*, 2016, June). See: www.theguardian.com/football/blog/2016/jun/27/iceland-england-euro-2016-triumph
3 From a pre-match television interview with Hans Backe (*RUV*, 2016, October 5).
4 Field notes.
5 An interview with Þorbjörn Jensson. "Leiðin á HM" (tv program; *Stöð 2.*, 2013, January).
6 "Ragnar um neikvæðar hliðar fótboltans" (article; *Visir.is.*, 2016, December). See: www.visir.is/ragnar-um-neikvaedu-hlidar-fotboltans – i-svithjod-og-danmorku-var-thad-mikilvaegasta-ad-laga-harid-/article/2016161229913.
7 "Lars: Strákarnir svindla ekki en þurfa samt að vera aðeins kaldari" (article; *Visir. is.*, 2016, June). See: www.visir.is/lars-strakarnir-svindla-ekki-en-thurfa-samt-ad-vera-adeins-kaldari/article/2016160618876
8 See Telseth, F. and Halldorsson, V. (forthcoming, "Size need not matter," to be published in a special issue of *Sport in Society*, Sept/Oct 2017).

References

Andersen, S.S. and Ronglan, L.T. (eds.) (2012). *Nordic elite sport: Same ambitions, different tracks*. Oslo: Universitetsforlaget.

Bale, J. (2007). Kenyan running before the 1968 Mexico Olympics. In Y. Pitsiladis, J. Bale, C. Sharp and T. Noakes (eds.), *East-African running: Towards a cross-disciplinary perspective* (pp. 11–23). London: Routledge.

Beamish, R. and Ritchie, I. (2006). *Fastest, highest, strongest: A critique of high-performance sport*. London: Routledge.

Billing, P., Franzén, M. and Peterson, T. (2004). Paradoxes of football professionalization in Sweden: A club approach. *Soccer and Society*, 5(1): 82–99.

Bloomfield, J. (2003). *Australia's sporting success: The inside story*. Kensington: University of New South Wales Press.

Collins, T. (2013). *Sport in capitalist society: A short history*. London: Routledge.

Corte, U. (2013). A refinement of collaborative circles: Resource mobilization and innovation in an emerging sport. *Social Psychology Quarterly*, 76(1): 25–51.

Eitzen, S. (2016). *Fair and foul: Beyond the myths and paradoxes of sport*. Lanham: Rowman & Littlefield.

Epstein, D. (2013). *The sports gene: Inside the science of extraordinary athletic performance*. New York: Penguin.

Finnbogason, G. ([1933]/1971). *Íslendingar: Nokkur drög að þjóðarlýsingu*. Reykjavík: Almenna Bókafélagið.

Guilianotti, R. and Robertson, R. (2004). A globalization of football: A study in the glocalization of the 'serious life.' *The British Journal of Sociology*, 55(4): 545–568.

Guttmann, A. (2004). *Sports: The first five millennia*. Amherst: University of Massachusetts Press.

Halldorsson, V., Helgason, A. and Thorlindsson, T. (2012). Attitude, commitment and motivation amongst Icelandic elite athletes. *International Journal of Sport Psychology*, 43(3): 241–254.

Halldorsson, V., Thorlindsson, T. and Katovich, M.A. (2014). The role of informal sport: The local context and the development of elite athletes. *Studies in Symbolic Interaction*, 42: 133–160.

Harper, D. (1987). *Working knowledge: Skill and community in a small shop*. Chicago: The University of Chicago Press.

Hill, M. (2007). *In pursuit of excellence*. London: Routledge.

Íþróttabandalag Reykjavíkur (2009). Ánægjuvogin: Leiðarvísir um áherslur í íþróttastarfi barna og ungmenna. Reykjavík: ÍBR.

Jarvie, G. (2003). Internationalism and sport in the making of nations. *Identities: Global Studies in Culture and Power*, 10: 537–551.

Mills, C.W. ([1951]/2002). *White collar: The American middle classes*. Oxford: Oxford University Press.

Nordal, S. (1987). *List og lífsskoðun III: Áfangar*. Reykjavík: Almenna Bókafélagið.

Peterson, T. (2008). The professionalization of sport in the Scandinavian countries. *Idrottsforum*. Available online at: www.idrottsforum.org/articles/peterson/peterson 080220.html.

Sennett, R. (2008). *The craftsman*. New Haven: Yale University Press.

Shogan, D.A. (1999). *The making of high-performance athletes: Discipline, diversity, and ethics*. Toronto: University of Toronto Press.

Steinarsson, S.Ó. (1994). *Strákarnir okkar: Saga landsliðsins í handknattleik 1950–1993*. Reykjavík: Fróði.

Thorlindsson, T. (1994). Skipper science: A note on the epistemology of practice and the nature of expertise. *Sociological Quarterly*, 35: 321–329.

Veblen, T. ([1914]/2006). *The instinct of workmanship, and the state of the industrial arts*. New York: Cosimo.

Wieting, S. (2015). *The sociology of hypocrisy: An analysis of sport and religion*. London: Routledge.

9   The advantages of small populations

In a small-scale society anonymity is impossible.

— Burton Benedict (1967, 51)

The international discourse on the achievements of the Icelandic national sport teams has been framed in terms of how such a small nation can achieve substantial results in modern sports. This discourse takes it for granted that being a small country, like Iceland, is a disadvantage in international sporting contests, which it is, in important ways. First, and most importantly, a small population decreases the chance of producing extraordinary talents or people with the appropriate physical attributes to excel in a given sport, and also of producing enough players with sufficient skills, at the same time, to build national teams that are competent at the international level. Second, very small societies lack the resources to host national professional league competitions, mainly because they do not have enough sports fans – spectators and other sports consumers – to bear the costs of such leagues (Coakley, 1998). Smaller nations have to build their elite sports from an amateur sports structure, resulting in disadvantages, compared to larger nations, in terms of elite sports training and expertise. Third, the costs of administration can be a burden for smaller societies, as they have to spend valuable financial resources which they could otherwise use on the sport itself on sports organization and infrastructure; in this, larger societies can benefit from economies of scale (Benedict, 1967).

The smallness of societies can, however, have advantages that can help tiny nations in sport as well as in other spheres (Benedict, 1967; Sam, 2016). Some research shows, for instance, that small societies are over-represented in elite sports while larger societies are under-represented (Carlson, 1988; MacDonald et al., 2009). According to Baldur Þórhallsson, one of the leading political scientists discussing small states, it is insufficient to look only at traditional variables, such as population size, sovereignty, political size and economic size to evaluate states' achievements (Thorhallsson, 2006). Other factors take on more relevance than the size of the population. The tight networks, multiplex ties (where people interact in multiple fields of activity, such as in sport, school and social gatherings) and informal communications contributing to constructing social capital within small societies can provide these networks with all kinds of influences and opportunities, which are missing in larger societies. Such "social capital is productive, making possible the achievement of certain ends that in its absence would not be possible" (Coleman, 1988, 98). This tightness seems to benefit Iceland. Various social and cultural elements have given Iceland the opportunity to use coordinated networks promoting play that the bigger nations lack owing to their size and bureaucratization of activity.

In this chapter I will specifically address how the small society of Iceland has become a source of advantage for it and its national sports teams and how the tight networks of the Icelandic community also function as social capital that encourages athletes and teams to play with a certain character.

Social networks and the facilitation of knowledge: "the village factor"

Iceland is a small society; frequently people in Iceland tend to find that they know each other or are related – this realization of relatedness has a strong impact, particularly for people within the same cultural or professional spheres. More generally, Icelanders interact according to the average of "one degree of separation." Benedict has noted that the strengths of such tight social networks lie in the interdependence of people within the network: "an outstanding characteristic of smallness is the coincidence or overlapping of roles so that individuals are tied to each other in many ways. This makes impartiality or impersonal role-relationships very difficult to maintain" (1967, 7).

Classical sociological theory proposes that individuals are embedded in cultures and relationships that shape them in numerous ways. For instance, individuals connect in terms of what is meaningful in the particular social context. They also conduct themselves according to the expectations in particular activities (Granovetter, 1986). Research supporting this general thesis has shown that achievements in various domains tend to be geographically concentrated in certain places (Powell et al., 2002; Von Hippel, 1994; Zucker, Darby and Armstrong, 1998). In such places, a knowledge of the way of how to do things spreads to others, in the form of socio-cultural influences. Such research indicates that it is through social networks (informal channels) that valuable knowledge is distributed, both explicitly and tacitly. Useful knowledge and practices are transferred, through imitation and emotional bonding, from one person to the next, as well as from the group to the individual. This diffusion of influence and information takes place more quickly and effectively between people and groups in smaller populations than in larger populations. Such diffusion also takes place on two levels, first through "strong ties" between people, which enhance communication and build trust and social capital (see Levin and Cross, 2004), and second through "weak ties," which build bridges between different groups (Granovetter, 1973).

Iceland is characterized by a network of strong ties. Its small population and tight networks – especially within a given subject (such as sports) – establish strong and unavoidable bonds between its members. In his analysis of the emergence of the thriving Icelandic popular music scene, Nick Prior (2015) concluded that its acknowledged substance was not related to Iceland's natural environment or the gene-stock of the Icelanders but to the social organization of ordinary Icelandic society. He identified what he termed "the village factor" as important in this respect, where musicians are in close contact with each other and share ideas and instruments and influence each other. Such sharing serves as a key explanation of the emergence of prominent Icelandic pop artists and bands. Thus, the smallness of Icelandic society builds tight social networks of people from the same field of action and people in these shared networks foster friendships and interdependence within the same social and cultural spheres. The friendships within and across networks have led to the emergence of a cultural "hot-spot" popular music scene.

In a similar fashion, the Icelandic sports scene is built on strong ties that facilitate a cultural sports hegemony, consisting of norms regarding how to play sports, which can be seen in all the aforementioned teams. The various Icelandic national teams draw on players who have known each other for years; they are friends or acquaintances, and are even blood related. There are, for instance, brothers in the national football and handball teams, as well as in the national handball and basketball teams. There are also two pairs of sisters in the women's basketball team. There were furthermore five players in the men's U19 football team who were in the same class in school.[1] Athletes are also part of a local (and profession-specific) network of sports, where they know each other, or of each other, from early on. In such a small community they cannot help establishing repeated co-presences since they belong to the same network. They are used to playing against each other, being selected for the same national youth teams, and catching a glimpse of each other at sporting events, at the cinema or in the street. This Icelandic familiarity is not necessarily the case in larger societies where the national team players only tend to meet around national team assignments. This Icelandic familiarity, interaction and interdependence of athletes towards each another builds connections and trust between players that are instrumental for the sharing of knowledge and for ascribing knowledge (Levin and Cross, 2004). Teams that consist of players from a network of strong ties will have a strong inclination to cultivate sound teamwork. One of the senior basketball players, Helgi Már Magnússon, described his feelings after he had retired from the national team in 2016 in those words:

> I think the main thing I will miss is being with these guys who I have known for such a long time . . . Meeting them and being with them was always a fixed point in my life, fooling around in the hotel rooms, laughing ourselves silly long into the night. This is what I will miss the most.[2]

Sports have strong roots in the local community. They draw on local traditions and social resources. The aforementioned Icelandic national teams have defined themselves by the culture they have shared, resulting in a specific Icelandic national team identity – across the various sports. They have learned to play "the Icelandic way," which has proven successful for other teams. However, cultural awareness, such as how they play, does not come automatically. Ideologies, methods, and practices need to be transferred between people and groups through "interlocks," particular individuals responsible for spreading specific cultural components from one group to the next, creating a culture that transcends any single group (Fine, 2012, 149). They create an interlocking culture through social networks. Networks are resources that connect people to something that is larger than themselves. No one person controls the networks but all can benefit from them through the ongoing interaction that occurs within them (Christakis and Fowler, 2009). Furthermore, knowledge travels from one group to the next through these interlocks, creating an ongoing interactional order within groups – a subculture – that comes to represent the local network. As Fine stated:

> Through these interlocks, group boundaries are bridged and cultural options extended, resulting in common discourse throughout the network by means of performance of shared knowledge. Once spread, cultural content may be localized within groups and then diffused material marked as their own. Each group develops a variant form of the culture of the larger network.
>
> (2012, 146)

The players influence one another directly, both explicitly and tacitly. This influence has been especially important in connection with the increased professionalization of sports in Iceland, where professional athletes influence other athletes and teach them the "tricks of the trade." Secretary-general of the National Olympic and Sports Association, Halldórsdóttir, says of such networks of connections between Icelandic athletes at the Olympic Games:

> The track and field athletes learned huge amounts from the swimmers. About discipline, food and sleep, the whole package. It rubbed off on them. Just knowing that the swimmers came to watch them, and vice versa. It gives you support; you are not just by yourself.

Handballer Stefánsson describes the knowledge transfer in the men's handball team more as a set of norms of appropriate behavior, rather than explicit teaching. The key players raise the bar and set new standards that other players adjust to. He argues that knowledge exchange happens tacitly through imitation:

> As things are at the moment, there are new men coming in. You don't always know how they tick. For example, Guðjón Valur; he has a certain attitude at practices. It's the way men are that rubs off, not so much what they say. Rather the way they are at practices. Then people start seeing: "Hey, that's it! That's what I need to do." They are not necessarily told this. . . . Like the bags that Guðjón and the other guys use. They have their kit and always take it with them to practices. So if someone new comes in, he will get the message, unconsciously, that he's only got a few months in which to start doing the same.

The national teams watch each other play, and they support each other, both privately, through meetings between the key players in different teams to learn from each other, and publicly, where they send good wishes to other teams in the run-up to each competition.[3] The teams make use of various tools which have proven useful to the other teams – such as "the Icelandic madness" mentality – and derive motivation from the games of other teams. Female handballer Guðmundsdóttir notes:

> They [the men's handball team] have got unbelievable results, which has influenced us in the women's team in many ways. For instance, in terms of handball 'know-how' and motivation. Their success has been a massive boost for us.

Also, the men's handball team, for instance, was motivated by the negative remarks by the Portuguese football player Ronaldo towards the Icelandic football team, and used them as "fuel" for their upcoming match against Portugal in the European handball play-offs.[4]

Mark Granovetter argues: "When a man changes jobs, he is not only moving from one network of ties to another, but also establishing a link between these" (1973, 1373). His statement emphasizes the importance of what has been termed "weak ties" for social networks. While strong ties bind individuals together into a group, weak ties bind groups together. The successful Icelandic professional athletes bring various types of expert knowledge from their professional teams back to their teammates in the national teams, as well as influencing the Icelandic sports scene generally. The increased number of Icelandic athletes playing professional sport in various countries abroad extends the local networks of Icelandic athletes to the professional world of sports by sharing information and best practices with their Icelandic friends and teammates who then adopt these practices (see Christakis and Fowler, 2009; Granovetter, 1973).

The argument presented here is that the strong ties that exist in the social networks of the small population of Iceland are important for interaction, knowledge exchange and the building of trust among Icelandic athletes. Thanks to these strong ties, the sporting community in Iceland is also able to thoroughly utilize global sports expertise through "weak ties": the pattern of transfer links in which the professional athletes function as "interlocks" between the professional sport worlds and the national teams from which the transfer continues to the local networks via the community of coaches and club athletes. This dialectical connection between strong and weak ties builds up cumulative knowledge that spreads to the wider Icelandic sports community.

Sharing important information is also the norm for Icelandic coaches. The Icelandic coaches that work at the professional level share information on training and tactics with other Icelandic coaches. "It's a small community and people learn from each other to some extent," says handball coach Guðmundsson. Successful coaching methods travel fast. Handball coach Jóhannesson argues that the coaching culture in Iceland is very open and helpful in this respect:

> This closeness, all the contact between the coaches is, I think, a huge advantage here in Iceland. The way we do this, it's very, very easy to get help from the next guy. I think this is a very strong point, and also with the coaches: we are very open to having everyone work together, even though we're playing against each other. If you need information of some type, it's a very simple matter to get it. I can see that this is very different from how things are in Austria, where I am coaching

now. There, each coach works in his own little corner. We are much more open in Iceland.

Communication is more open because the coaches have common backgrounds; they rely on pasts that each recognize, even if they have not experienced them directly with each other (Katovich and Couch, 1992). Jóhannesson says: "I know Alfreð; he was my coach. I played with Dagur and also with Erlingur Richards. I think this also makes us open in our dealings with each other. Within the group, we talk to each other."

This commonality of pasts and their usefulness also takes place in the day-to-day activities in the sport clubs. Sports broadcaster Jónsson says: "Most of the sports clubs here cover several sports. It's an easy matter for a football coach to go over and watch a handball practice session, or vice versa. Just to see what people are doing, if they are interested." This is not necessarily the case elsewhere, according to the foreign football experts, who report that their coaches are more used to keeping useful information to themselves. The Icelandic handball expert Sigmundsson, who lives in Norway, described the lack of communication between the Norwegian men's and women's national handball teams as follows:[5]

> Yet in Norway, the men's national handball team doesn't follow what the women's national team is doing, even though they are World, Olympic and European champions. There's a certain rivalry between the two of them. It's amazing to see that they have no interest in seeing what they are doing, how they build themselves up for a competition or how they get through it. It's a bit weird. You can learn from something that that goes well and is successful. It's part of the way we are, being a small country and all that. But it's much less the case in Norway, being such a big, spread-out country, with more competition.

Shorter ways to the top

Another important element regarding the smallness of Icelandic society relates to the premise that the road to the top in Icelandic sports is shorter than in larger countries, which itself gives local hopefuls more of a stimulus, and more realistic opportunities to gain prestige. The motivation and self-confidence that people in Iceland have to reach the elite level – whether it is in sport, music or something else – is in part enhanced by the smallness of Icelandic society. The small networks of social connections in Iceland provide everyone with a link to someone who has been successful in some field and therefore perceive that they have the opportunity to do it as well. Increased numbers of professional players, playing abroad in recent years, brings the dream of also making it closer to other Icelandic athletes. Footballer Skúlason notes:

> These guys I've known since way back and played handball with – they are doing brilliantly in major competitions. When you see that, you think: "I can do that too." We also have a lot of good footballers. I don't think it's a matter of standing in front of the television and saying "Hey, we can do that too." I think it's more something unconscious, the feeling that we can do it too.

This closeness to the people who have "made it" – the role models – motivates young players to do more. Footballer Finnbogason reflects on the inspiration when players around him – his friends – started to land professional deals abroad:

> It struck me: "Listen, they're doing that, why shouldn't I be able to? If I get down to a bit of work and polish up my technique. Do that little bit extra. I could be in the same position."

In smaller societies the opportunities for aspiring young players in sports to reach the elite level are in some ways more within reach, and therefore more realistic, than for young players in larger populations.

The scarcity of available players in Iceland can further be seen to have helped young Icelandic players. The clubs have only a limited number of adult players available for their teams so they have to look to the younger players. This can be seen from the fact that younger players experience repeated opportunities to play with adults from an early age. In other words, the teams must make full use of what they have. Youngsters have the chance to play at the senior level, make mistakes, learn from failures and develop into senior players by playing with, and learning from, them. The fact that the youngsters are, and feel, needed – and not disposable – further strengthens their loyalty and commitment to those teams (Sennett, 2008, 10). In countries with larger numbers of potential players, most younger players don't get such repeated opportunities, but are replaced by the next talented hopefuls if they don't make good use of their one-off opportunities, according to a foreign football expert interviewed for this book.

The chance that aspiring young players have to be selected for elite groups or to youth national teams, or to be in the media and to become recognized as athletes with a reputation, is also much greater in smaller societies than in larger – even though the players in the larger societies may have more talent. Those who do well in small societies are instantly recognized by the public, which gives them a motivational boost. Halldórsdóttir raises this point:

> You're probably going to be a much smaller cog in a much bigger machine in a big country. And the ordinary people who achieve top results, you don't even know their names in big countries. [Here] you know their names. And even a lot lower down the achievement scale here in Iceland . . . When we get these people, they are very prominent in the small population. If you are a star here, your reputation reaches everyone in the country.

Thus, the importance of each individual is perceived as being greater among the citizens in such a small society than in larger ones. The smallness of Icelandic society has enhanced the feelings of young hopefuls in sports that the road to the top is both shorter and more easily traveled than if they were part of a much larger community and has also meant that the ambitious decisions taken at the organizational level have raised the confidence and determination of Icelandic athletes in international competition. Thus, Iceland has managed to utilize its players' resources effectively.

Theatrical intelligibility: the importance of social capital

The general public has a limited understanding of the technical and tactical dimensions of sports (Coakley, 1998). For instance, understanding of what counts as a good game strategy or good defensive work is not within the scope of knowledge of the general spectator or television viewer. In order to capture the interests of the masses, sports therefore have to make appeals to various onlookers, mainly by appealing to their emotions. They have to establish interest that can be "communicated in terms intelligible to others" (see Fine, 2015, 67). This appeal was the case in the 1972 World Championship chess match between the American Bobby Fischer and the Soviet Boris Spassky,[6] which in the heyday of the Cold War was represented as the battle between West and East. Despite the public's limited knowledge of the inner workings of the game of chess, the event appealed to emotions even of new chess players and has been labeled as one of the key sporting contests of the twentieth century. This sort of appeal and subsequent popularity is an example of what Fine referred to as "theatrical intelligibility" (2015, 67).

To understand the meaning of sport for Iceland as a nation, it is important to address the theatrical intelligibility of sport for the Icelanders. As illustrated above (see Chapter 3), Icelandic sports associations and clubs were in part established to help fight for the independence of Iceland from the colonial power, Denmark. Anthropologist Eduardo Archetti argues in this vein that baseball was seen as an important "weapon of resistance" against Spanish colonialism in Cuba that helped the nation towards independence (Archetti, 1999, 192). It was as important for Norway to beat its larger neighbor Sweden (Goksøyr, 1998), as it was for Iceland to beat its former ruler Denmark. Sports helped the Icelandic nation to feel independent from Denmark, as is illustrated by the words of an elderly man who came onto the field after Iceland beat Denmark for the first time in handball in 1969 and declared with tears in his eyes: "Finally we are independent" (Sigurpálsson, 2012, 490). Thus, Iceland's late achievement of independence, together with its small population, geographical isolation and economic progress in the late twentieth century, combined to fuel the spirits of Icelanders to show their worth on the world stage, to be a nation among nations. "Icelanders are obsessed with earning approval from outside the country. We want foreigners to signal their approval of our abilities and our existence," argues sports broadcaster Jónsson. In this context, Icelanders have been compelled to look beyond their own borders, whether this is in sports, business or the arts. Sports historian Lúðvíksson argues:

> Sports were a very powerful force in stimulating Icelanders' sense of nationhood. At first, after independence, we were still very insecure. We didn't know where we stood in relation to other nations. The sports victories that were won counted for a very great deal . . . they gave birth to national heroes and models that showed us we could be the equals of others.

Throughout the twentieth century, Icelanders were somewhat burdened by an "elder-brother" complex. Whenever a famous foreigner mentioned Iceland in an interview it made them proud, and when an Icelander achieved international recognition – however small – the nation took notice. Icelanders prided themselves in being the best in the world in various domains, though these records were frequently expressed in *per capita* terms. International contests, such as beauty contests, the Eurovision Song Contest, strongmen's contests and traditional sporting contests thus provided the nation with an opportunity to fulfill its needs not only by belonging but also, on occasion, by beating larger and more prestigious nations. It was tiny Iceland against the rest of the world, David against Goliath. Live coverage of these contests transformed them into modern drama – rather like a modern form of the Icelandic sagas – capturing the attention of the whole population, which watched and was emotionally engaged in the contests in question. There was much at stake: the nation's identity.

In this context, social capital theory draws our attention to the impact of the social and cultural context on sporting performance at the macro level

(Coleman, 1988; Putnam, 2000). Since the elite athletes are closely tied to their extended families and their local networks back home, ordinary Icelanders feel they are connected to the players who play the game and that they play a part in the achievements of the teams on the field. Halldórsdóttir states: "The national pride is huge when our boys and girls are playing . . . we feel like we own a part in their success, because they are so close to us." This is evident in the massive interest of the Icelandic population in international competitions where representatives of Iceland take part. Sport contests as well as the Eurovision Song Contest can attract 80–90% of the population in the audience of the live television coverage, which is by far the highest figure in Europe according to sports broadcaster Jónsson. Everyone supports the national sports teams when they do well. The men's football team captain, Aron Einar Gunnarsson, said:

> Icelanders are interested in all sports, and particularly the big competitions we participate in. And when they are played here, everyone goes crazy. We are very much aware of this; we enjoy it and try to use this support to our advantage.[7]

The ordinary Icelander feels that he or she is connected to the elite athletes representing the nation on the field and shows support and interest in what they are doing. Footballer Viðarsdóttir spoke of the difference in this respect between Iceland and Sweden, where she played as a professional:

> Icelanders are of course quite incredibly close-knit when things go well. Everyone knows that; it's just how we are as a nation. We are always aware of who are our brightest stars. When we got into the European Championships, everyone congratulated us. People who didn't know us personally at all. Everyone knew what was going on. I've played a bit abroad, in Sweden. I could make embarrassing mistakes in a game there and no one would notice. No one came and rubbed it in in the shop the next day. No one knew who I was and no one really cared at all one way or the other. Here you really get to know about it if you have not been up to scratch, and also you get the praise when you do well.

In the small-scale society of Iceland, sport stars are identified as one of the people, and the nation supports them wholeheartedly, as footballer Skúlason describes:

> We are such a very tiny nation. Everyone knows everyone else somehow. You can't go out to an ice-cream parlour without meeting someone you know. When it comes to support, we really go to town. The support we get! Everyone's hooked on sport in Iceland.

The national teams take this identification to a new level, above that of the individual clubs. It doesn't matter for the players or supporters, whether a player from KR or Valur scores for the national team: what matters is that the team is doing well. This is not always the case in regards to all national teams. Basketball player Bæringsson further reflects on the support given by the Icelandic spectators attending matches in the European finals in basketball:

> Somehow, everyone involved in basketball in Iceland was there. Naturally it helped us a great deal. I could almost tell you the names of the people in the stands. The bonds are so strong that you really feel the desire to succeed for someone other than yourself. You're not likely to lapse into some negative attitude. The fact that all those people have turned out makes the whole experience so incredible. Group singing and all that is something you never forget as long as you live.

It is estimated that over 30,000 Icelandic spectators attended the European Championship finals in men's football in 2016. The relatives, friends and friends of friends of the athletes showed up and showed support. "You know almost half the people in the grandstand. There aren't many teams that have supporters like that," said football player Kári Árnason at the European Championship in 2016.[8]

Interest in sports is not sport specific when it comes to the national teams. Icelanders tend to watch and support their representatives, in any sport whatever, when they are playing in big tournaments, even though they don't follow the sport or know the rules of the game. Footballer Viðarsdóttir further states:

> It's so easy to get people interested. Take the men's basketball team, for instance. I never watch basketball and don't even know the rules. But I watched every single match. Why? Well, it was made interesting. Of course, I am Icelandic and am interested in sport.

The argument presented here is that the general interest in sport in Iceland, along with the need of the members of the small island nation to prove themselves on the world stage, works as a collective motivation found affecting almost all generations, groups and individuals in Icelandic society. This massive national interest and support help the teams in the field of action, both in terms of perceived interest and support and also in terms of social control, as sports broadcaster Guðmundsson – whose son plays in the national handball team – argues:

> Everyone says it would be a lousy character who wouldn't want to play in the national team. They hardly even have any insurance in the

national team, but there's something deep inside them that makes them want to do it. They have to turn up. Caught in the net; that's how it is. They want to acquit themselves reasonably well, do their bit. It's just something in us, the way we are.

According to Coleman (1988) social control facilitates certain actions and constrains other through social norms and expectations. It is in this context that the interest of the Icelandic people in its national teams works as a social capital for the teams. The players want to do well, not only for their ambitious and sometimes egoistic reasons as elite athletes, but also for the people back home. Since they are so closely linked to the people back home they are prompted not to lose face in front of their kin (Goffman, [1959]/1990). One football coach said: "If you don't do well, you'll be letting your own families down." The national team players want to belong with the people back home and they want to make them proud. And when they come home, they want to hold their heads up high in front of their people. Handballer Stefánsson reflects on the importance of playing well, for the nation, in the big tournaments that are held in January almost every year:

> I suppose it's a kind of pride, really. A sort of national pride. There are external factors, but also these internal ones. I mean: you have family and how you do will be talked about. People are watching. You know it matters to them. Even if this is in January and maybe many times again every year, it still matters to people how you do this January. And you've heard it many times before, and you hear it now too: it matters to people. You think, maybe: 'Why is some guy in Egilsstaðir or Búðardalur going to be watching this? Will it make his day? Does he care? Will anything change for him if we do well?' You realize that you have a kind of responsibility there. You know you'll never actually meet this farmer, or bloke, whoever he is. But yes, it does matter.

This kind of informal social control further compels the players to keep their feet on the ground despite their international recognition and success. There is no room for "big shots" in the Icelandic teams, as basketball player Stefánsson argues:

> It comes down to this closeness. You are with someone on the pitch who you're connected to in some way. We have had lots of superstars through the years, but they are all "down to earth." They could just as easily behave like Ronaldo here in Iceland, since they have everything for it. But they don't. Part of this is that their families live here; either they live here or have all their extended family here.

The internationally experienced sports broadcaster Jónsson has noted this sense of humility in how the Icelandic athletes present themselves in interviews. He comments:

This is why all superstar conduct is really unknown among people in Iceland who excel in any field whatever. You just don't find it. People are just part of the community. If someone stops Eiður Smári in the street [the most famous Icelandic footballer], he will just talk to them and then go ahead and pay the same five hundred krónur as the next man in the queue. This is something you don't see in bigger places. You don't get anything out of being a star in Iceland. No one is going to give you a car.

It is furthermore the norm in Icelandic sports that national players make themselves available for national games. Despite their tight schedules with their professional teams – and even against the will of their employees, and despite the physical tiredness, the mental challenges, the great deal of travel and the fact that they derive no monetary gain for playing with the national team – they still show up. Almost without exception. Handball coach Guðmundsson states: "I have always found these guys ready to make sacrifices. They nearly always come forward to play for the national team." This addresses the same point: the national team players are prepared to make a sacrifice. They don't want to let each other down and they don't want to let the people back home down.

The inter-relationships of the national team athletes as well as the ties of the team's players to the larger Icelandic community have strengthened the morale in the national teams and also the bonds between the national teams and the Icelandic nation. Thus, the impact of the small-scale society has played an important part in the making and motivation of those teams, giving them certain advantages over teams from larger and more diverse populations as regards team cohesion, personal sacrifice and self-confidence and a sense of purpose over and beyond that of merely winning or losing: playing for the folks back home.

Notes

1 "25% leikmanna U19 ára landsliðsins koma úr sama bekk" (article; *Fotbolti.net.*, 2014, March). See: www.fotbolti.net/news/06-03-2014/25-leikmanna-u19-ara-landslidsins-koma-ur-sama-bekk
2 "Helgi Már: Á eftir að sakna hláturskastanna á hótelherberginu" (article; *Visir.is.*, 2016, February). See: www.visir.is/helgi-mar–a-eftir-ad-sakna-hlaturskastanna-a-hotelherberginu/article/2016160219158
3 "Fótboltastrákarnir senda handboltastrákunum kveðju" (article; *Visir.is.*, 2015, January). *Visir.is*. See: www.visir.is/fotboltastrakarnir-senda-handboltastrakunum-kvedju/article/2016160119210

120   *How culture affects sport*

"Myndband: Íslenska körfuknattleiksliðið sendi strákunum fallega kveðju" (article: *433.is.*, 2015, September). See: http://433.is/deildir/island/myndband-islenska-korfuknattleikslandslidid-sendi-strakunum-fallega-kvedju/

4 "Ronaldo búinn að kveikja í landsliðinu" (article; *Visir.is.*, 2016, June). See: www.visir.is/ronaldo-buinn-ad-kveikja-i-handboltalandslidinu/article/2016160619213

5 An Icelander, Thorir Hergeirsson, is the head coach of the Norwegian women's national handball team.

6 The match was held in Iceland in 1972 and is often referred to as "the match of the century."

7 "Aron Einar: Það eru allir bilaðir heima og við fögnum því" (article, *Visir.is.*, 2016, June). See: www.visir.is/aron-einar-thad-eru-allir-biladir-heima-og-vid-fognum-thvi/article/2016160619045#

8 "Kári Árnason: Maður þekkir helminginn af fólkinu í stúkunni" (article; *Visir.is.*, 2016, June). See: www.visir.is/kari-arnason – madur-thekkir-helminginn-af-folkinu-i-stukunni/article/2016160619225

References

Archetti, E.P. (1999). *Masculinities: Football, polo and the tango in Argentina*. Oxford: Berg.

Benedict, B. (ed.) (1967). *Problems of smaller territories*. London: The Athlone Press.

Carlson, R. (1988). The socialization of elite tennis players in Sweden: An analysis of the players' background and development. *Sociology of Sport Journal*, 5: 241–256.

Christakis, N.A. and Fowler, J.A. (2009). *Connected: The surprising power of our social networks and how they shape our lives*. New York: Little, Brown & Company.

Coakley, J. (1998). *Sport in society: Issues and controversies*. Boston: McGraw-Hill.

Coleman, J. (1988). Social capital in the creation of human capital. *American Journal of Sociology*, 94: 95–120.

Fine, G.H. (2012). *Tiny publics: A theory of group action and culture*. New York: Russell Sage Foundation.

Fine, G.H. (2015). *Players and pawns: How chess builds community and culture*. Chicago: Chicago University Press.

Goffman, E. ([1959]/1990). *The presentation of self in everyday life*. London: Penguin Books.

Goksøyr, M. (1998). Football, development and identity in a small nation: Football culture, spectators and playing styles in twentieth century Norway. *Football Studies*, 1: 37–47.

Granovetter, M. (1973). The strength of weak ties. *American Journal of Sociology*, 78(6): 11360–1380.

Granovetter, M. (1986). Economic action and social structure. The problem of embeddedness. *American Journal of Sociology*, 91: 481–510.

Katovich, M.A. and Couch, C.J. (1992). The nature of social pasts and their use as foundations for situated action. *Symbolic Interactionism*, 15(1): 25–47.

Levin, D.Z. and Cross, R. (2004). The strength of weak ties you can trust: The mediating role of trust in effective knowledge transfer. *Management Science*, 50(11): 1477–1490.

MacDonald, D.J., Cheung, M., Cote, J. and Abernethy, B. (2009). Place but not date of birth influences the development and emergence of athletic talent in American football. *Journal of Applied Sport Psychology*, 21(1): 80–90.

Powell, W.W., Koput, K.W., Bowie, J.I. and Smith-Doerr, L. (2002). The spatial clustering of science and capital: Accounting for biotech firm-venture capital relationships. *Regional Studies*, 36: 291–305.

Prior, N. (2015). "It's a social thing, not a nature thing": Popular music practices in Reykjavik, Iceland. *Cultural Sociology*, 9(1): 81–98.

Putnam, R. (2000). *Bowling alone: The collapse and revival of American community*. New York: Simon & Schuster.

Sam, M. (2016). Youth sport policy in small nations. In K. Green and A. Smith (eds.), *Routledge handbook of youth sport* (pp. 535–542). London: Routledge.

Sennett, R. (2008). *The craftsman*. New Haven: Yale University Press.

Sigurpálsson, B.V. (2012). Þjóðarsálin fer á flug. In S.J. Lúðvíksson (ed.), *Íþróttabókin: Saga og samfélag í 100 ár* (pp. 484–501). Reykjavík: ÍSÍ.

Thorhallsson, B. (2006). The size of states in the European Union: Theoretical and conceptual perspectives. *European Integration*, 28(1): 7–31.

Von Hippel, E. (1994). "Sticky information" and the locus of problem solving: Implications for innovation. *Management Science*, 40(4): 429–439.

Zucker, L.G., Darby, M.R. and Armstrong, J. (1998). Geographically localized knowledge: Spillovers or markets? *Economic Inquiry*, 36(1): 65–86.

Part V
How it all comes together

10 Conclusion

The secret is that there is no secret.

– Rasmus Ankersen (2012, 39)

Iceland's collective sporting success cannot be explained by individual-level, sport-specific, linear cause-and-effect relationships. It is founded on broader cultural conditions that have been favorable for Iceland over the last decade, which individual sports have utilized effectively, enabling them to rise to new levels. The sporting successes of the Icelandic national teams are not easy to explain, however. Excellence and achievement are parts of mundane norms and customs of everyday life in which athletes partake, even when they are not aware of the significance of those norms and customs (Chambliss, 1988). Social relationships are fundamentally complex, and to complicate things even further, they are built on traditions, values and norms that do not have a substantive existence in the material world and are not visible to the human eye. In this book, I have used a sociological perspective to explore Iceland's success in sports, highlighting the important socio-cultural components that exist in and around the teams. In the previous chapters, I have described, step-by-step, various aspects of how the sporting successes of Iceland's national teams are cultural product. In this final chapter, I will build on those former chapters and propose a theory to illustrate how important socio-cultural components come together and have complemented each other in this respect. I examine how they are activated – or "turned on" – under specific circumstances, as when Icelandic athletes play for the national teams. Some of these components reside in the local national culture, while others lie in the global development of sports and sporting expertise, as well as in opportunities that have opened up in the global world of sports. These social components and relationships represent *the general* within all *the particular* teams analyzed in this book.

First, however, it is important to state that it is neither my argument that Icelanders are genuinely better in sports than anybody else, nor that Icelanders are better equipped for sports in terms of physiological attributes or genetics (the notion that the successful athletes come from Viking stock), than anybody else. I do not believe that the sports system and organization of sport in Iceland is better than sport systems in other countries; though it has been well suited for its national sport teams in recent years, it has its strengths (particularly the youth sports system) and weaknesses, just like every other sports system in the world. I also do not argue that there is some unique "Icelandic way of playing sport." Important team concepts, such as teamwork and teams that build on strong characters, are not unique to Icelandic athletes and teams. Handball coach Guðmundsson, who steered the Danish team to winning the Olympic gold medal in 2016, argues in this respect:

> I must admit that Danish players are in most cases ready to work hard. They have good attitudes, just like the players from Iceland. Icelanders always think that they are best in everything they do, but it's not like that. I have coached players from various countries. They are generally ready to work hard; this is not unique to Icelanders. . . . You can see teams like Croatia, they are ready to do everything they can for the national team. You see the Germans now. Iceland is not the only nation ready to put in the fight.

Finally, I do not argue that the major socio-cultural components that reside in the local culture in Iceland and help form the attitude and interest towards sport, such as national pride, a culture of play, and the general interest of the population in sport are unique to Iceland. They exist in most societies, but to different degrees at different times. It is, however, interesting that all the successful Icelandic teams achieved their success at the same time and that all the teams are built on similar characteristics and a similar style of play. My argument for applying a socio-cultural analysis on those successes rests on these facts.

The importance of balance

The central argument put forward in this book is that it has been important for Iceland how various social, cultural and historical elements have come together in recent years, which has provided Iceland with the foundations to punch above its weight at the international sports stage. Thus, it is important, in this respect, to acknowledge the underlying characteristics of sports in Iceland, such as: the general value of sport in Icelandic society, which sees sport as an important socializing agent and gives rise to massive youth sport participation; the interest of Icelanders in sports, which is built on reference to the Viking ancestry as to Iceland's fight for independence and functions as social capital and social control for the national teams; and the amateur approach to sport in Iceland, which still prevails over the professionalism and commercialism that characterizes most elite sports.

One of the key arguments of this analysis is that the fundamental elements on which Icelandic sports have been based since the early days – in fact, they can even be traced back to the sagas (see Wieting, 2015) – are still present in the national teams today. Most importantly, the emphasis on an amateur approach to sport encourages participants to see sport as play. This amateur approach to sport consists of sport being perceived as a social activity to be played with friends, played for honor with an emphasis on displaying good character and played emotionally and competitively. These elements still form the heart of Icelandic sports and build a common core among the successful Icelandic national teams. Additionally, Icelandic sports have, in recent years, added more professionalism on top of these amateur components (see Chapter 4). Greater professional expertise has been vital for the development of Icelandic sports in order for them to face competition at the highest level.

The achievements of the Icelandic national teams can be viewed in terms of how the right balance between amateurism and professionalism has emerged (Peterson, 2008). While the teams have adopted a more professional and organized way of playing sport, they have retained an important element of their amateur approach, as they still play "with their hearts." Thus, Icelandic teams have in recent years become more professional, but not too professional. This has given the Icelandic national teams an important edge over some of their more professional opponents, which sometimes lack character and teamwork.[1] Icelandic sports have, in this sense, gained the best of both worlds.

Another important component for the successes of the Icelandic teams is the interesting dualism between collectivism and individualism that resides in the Icelandic character. On the one hand, the strong collectivism in Icelandic society is apparent in the teams, which build their play on strong and cohesive teamwork in which players make individual sacrifices for the team. On the other hand, the individualistic spirit in the Icelandic character can be seen as a key driver of Icelandic athletes' ambition. They are generally known to be self-reliant, reliable, hard workers and of robust character. This mixture of the communal and individual elements has been important for the Icelandic national teams, which build on effective teamwork based on individual responsibility.

Further connections and balances can be identified in the combination of disparate elements. For instance, the different scales of "amateur-professional" and "communal-individual" complement each other. The way

Icelanders approach sport as play is representative of an amateur sports culture built from the communal culture in which the athletes belong. One wouldn't exist without the other. Together the amateur and the communal cultures combine to form teams that represent great teamwork, friendship and the joy of playing. Likewise, the individualistic approach to sport, which the Icelanders possess, is well suited to professional sport, which seeks ambitious, reliable and mentally strong players. Thus, the individualistic spirit of the Icelanders complements the professional approach to sport: foreign professional sports teams seek Icelandic athletes for their character rather than their sporting talent.

Other important cultural influences are also at play in this dialectical context, such as how do the mutual loyalties and commitments of teamwork hold in the commercialized world of elite sports, which tends to intensify individualistic tendencies? In the specific case of the Icelandic national teams, the smallness of the close-knit Icelandic society functions as a form of social control (Coleman, 1988). Such control holds many of those cultural components together in the right balance. The small society, its interest in sports and the pride of its people combine to "turn on" "the Icelandic madness" in Icelandic teams, reinforcing their concepts of honor and the defense of their reputation, and hence of the nation's reputation too (Wieting, 2015). Thus, the egoistic motivations, which Icelanders possess – and which are further fueled by increased global commercialism and idolization of elite sport – are constrained by the collective social control exercised by the small society. This social control encourages the players to be humble, show good character and to forego their own egos for the team and the nation. The players do not want to come back home to their families and friends "shamefaced" by having displayed the "wrong" attitude (Goffman, [1967]/2008, 8). They want to avoid public humiliation and "play along" with the cultural expectations of how to behave in those settings. These controlling effects of social capital on the behavior of national team players would be more difficult to achieve in larger and more impersonal societies (Coleman, 1988).

It is further interesting to note how similar cultural elements can produce different results in different contexts. The cases of the Icelandic "Vikings" in sport and in business provide ideal examples of this. Both the national team athletes (the "sporting Vikings") and the bankers and investors (the "Outvasion Vikings" discussed in Chapter 3) were in part driven by comparable egoistic motivations. This motivation was, and is, to preserve their positive self-identity and status in the local community (see Goffman, [1967]/2008, 268). The athletes can achieve such positive self-identity and status by showing good character and achieving good results on the sports field. The Outvasion Vikings, on the other hand, achieved it by showing off their success, most notably by gaining wealth and displaying it in materialistic terms, such as by having fancy cars, yachts, and private jets or by signing celebrities such as Elton John to sing at their birthday parties. This is what Veblen termed "conspicuous consumption" ([1899]/1970). Thus, what the Icelandic athletes and bankers have in common is that their actions are driven forward by desire to make an impressive self-presentation towards their fellow neighbors and countrymen.

I argued above that what holds together the aforementioned cultural components, and is important for Icelandic sports, is that the Icelanders want to preserve their honor by showing good character and make the people back home proud. This desire contributes to the particularly strong character and teamwork in the teams. However, the Icelandic bankers and investors, whose recklessness was partly to blame for the 2008 financial meltdown in Iceland (discussed in Chapter 3), did not show the same characteristics as the athletes, despite coming from the same social background. One of the key reasons for the different outcomes lies in the difference in context (Thorlindsson, 2011). First, the worlds of sports and business are two different cultures. Each is based on different traditions, networks, values, and processes of socialization, and such differences create different meanings for participants in the different professional spheres. Business has, however, adopted (and exploited) some of the concepts that build the ideology of sports – such as teamwork, attitude, commitment and contest (see Collins, 2013, 120) – but works towards different ends. Each of the differences resides in the different social contexts (see Mixa and Vaiman, 2015). Second, differences exist and are associated with whether the performances of actors in different contexts are *public* or *private*. Sporting contests are transparent in the sense that each time the athletes enter the sporting arena they become publicly exposed. Their performance shows their worth. They cannot "fake" their way to success and there is no place to hide. Not only do they represent themselves and their nations, but their families as well, as their family names are displayed on the back of their shirts. When there is much at stake, the athletes must publicly show their professional character. In the business world, on the other hand, there are no such clear-cut and ongoing measures of character or success. People can act as if they are successful and make an impressive self-presentation, even if there is no substance behind their perceived success. Things are not always what they seem to be, as was the case with Iceland's "Outvasion Vikings" (Durrenberger and Palsson, 2015).

Thus, while the athletes may have been tempted to act more individualistically – by the huge incentives that often accompany individualist behavior in elite sports – they were inclined to show the "right" character and constrain their individualistic motivations in favor of the team. Businessmen, however, are not faced with such evident evaluations of their actions.

Business ownership and individual actions become obscured in complex networks of the business world. Businessmen can therefore be more easily tempted to act individualistically than can athletes. Their self-interested actions do not elicit the same immediate responses from their countrymen as is the case with the national team athletes. It is only through rare disclosures that their "self-interested" and sometimes illegal actions become known to the public. An example of the individualistic inclination of prominent Icelanders surfaced in the disclosures of the Panama Papers.[2] The Panama leak showed that no nation had more people who had put their money into secret bank-accounts in offshore tax-havens than the Icelanders.[3] "The unique selling point of offshore companies is that they provide anonymity" argue Obermayer and Obermaier, the leading journalists who exposed the Panama scandal (2016, 11). This example highlights the temptation to indulge in isolated individualistic behavior in contexts such as the business world (Hofstede, Hofstede and Minkov, 2010). In the sports world this temptation is restrained; an athlete is in the public eye most of the time, and any underhand conduct would result in a loss of face both in the estimation of the other team members and that of the public at home. This is especially applicable to such a small society such as Iceland.

This discussion of the different constraints on "Vikings" in the spheres of sport, on the one hand, and business, on the other, illustrates the complexity of how social structures work and influence individual and collective action. Above, I have illustrated some key social relationships that lie at the core of the Icelandic teams. These relationships serve as examples of how important social components came together and how they were influential in the building of a sports culture that emphasizes the importance of showing good character in sports and creates teams that draw on collective effort and strong teamwork. Many other social factors exist in this context but they are beyond the scope of this book.

Potential threats to the Icelandic model

Apparently, the attitude towards sport as play is something that has contrasted Iceland from some of its opponents' nations in team sport where the successful Icelandic elite sports have not been built up around money, as is the case in most elite sports (Collins, 2013). With increased capital invested in professional sports – which leads to increased commercialization and glorification of modern sports – elite sports have lost some of the fundamental elements of successfully playing team sport, dropping the approach to sport as play in favor of a more mechanical approach to sport as work (see a critique of the mechanical approach in Harper, 1987; Mills, [1951]/2002; Sennett, 2008). However, the Icelandic teams still retain some of the values associated with the amateur ethos of sport as play *even when competing* in elite sports. These values have been one of the key factors in the Icelandic national sport teams, which the more professional teams may lack in some respects. However, recent developments could pose a threat to some of the core elements in Icelandic sports, such as the approach to sport as play. It can be argued that increasing professionalism in sport, with the accompanying commercialism, individualism on the part of players and idolization of sports on the part of the public, poses the biggest threat to the equilibrium that has been important for Icelandic sports in recent years (see Huizinga, [1938]/1971; Veblen, [1915]/1964). The decline of successful sporting traditions, such as of Kenyan middle- and long-distance runners and Norwegian men's football, state the case.[4]

A few instances may be cited specifically regarding commercialization. In July 2016, the Icelandic government quadrupled the amount that the state provides to the main sporting authority in Iceland, the National Olympic and Sports Association,[5] to be spent on elite sports. It is scheduled to rise each year over the next four years, to become 17 times higher in 2020 than it was in 2011 – but even then, it will still be proportionally below the level of official support in the Scandinavian nations. In this regard, some indications of the damaging effects of increased money on offer to players in the national teams have begun to surface in Icelandic national team sports. After the men's football team qualified for the European finals there was hot debate among the Icelandic players as to how to re-negotiate the distribution of the bonus payments earned by the team for qualifying for the championship. This renegotiation took some time to conclude, and in the end it didn't have lasting effects on the team, or on team morale – perhaps because this was the first time the team had reached a major competition and the players didn't want to miss this historic opportunity. The sudden influx of money has, however, created new problems and challenges that the Icelandic national teams have not had to address before and that have the potential to disrupt the normal chemistry that the athletes are used to in the context of their national teams. Such instances of payment negotiations can be considered as an "alarm bell" for Icelandic sports.

Further, one prominent example of the modernization and professionalization of Icelandic sports, which could pose a threat to how Icelanders play sport, is the proliferation of indoor football halls. While some see indoor halls as essential for improving the Icelandic football players' technical skills, others argue that the halls may pose dangers to the already successful way Icelanders play football. This argument rests on the notion that if future generations of Icelandic football players play indoor football over the course of the long winters in Iceland, instead of playing outdoors, they will miss the opportunity to practice in harsh conditions in the wintertime, and run the risk of losing the characteristics on which their successful teams are based. Þorgrímur Þráinsson reflects on this trend:

> The football halls are very good for making sure people feel comfortable at practices and can work on their technique and so on. But they take away the experience of being out in the rain and wind and snow, and playing on gravel, and the need to be tough and never give up. Things have gotten a lot softer. I'm afraid that going soft like this could make us end up in a bad way in four years' time and face a real challenge we find we aren't ready for. I think there would be more of a chance that people would just give up, more than there is with the guys we have today.

It has still to be seen what effect increased professionalism will have for Icelandic elite athletes and the Icelandic national teams in the future. Ideally, increased funding will help individual athletes to reach the next level and Icelandic teams to stabilize themselves among the best, but it could also make Icelandic sport more mechanical, professional and calculating, where the danger is that the "heart and soul" of Icelandic sports will be lost along the way. Basketball coach Pedersen concludes:

> If money were involved it would almost ruin it for them, because there is so much pride in playing for Iceland. They are playing with their best friends, it's not a job, it's something they enjoy doing. They like to be with their friends and to do what they love.

Concluding remarks

There is no clear-cut answer to the question proposed at the beginning of this book: what factors allowed a tiny nation such as Iceland to beat England in the 2016 men's European football finals? The argument presented here is that many socio-cultural components were important. How they came together at a certain point in time was essential for the Icelandic teams to be able to emerge on the international sports scene. Many of these elements have been discussed in this book. However, my attempt to investigate the achievements do not cover all the relevant topics. Thus, it is neither a holistic account of the case in question nor a fully developed analysis of the elements under discussion. It is first and foremost an attempt to turn our attention towards understanding some of the aspects of a national sporting success through a socio-cultural analysis – to shift the focus from an individual-level analysis to analysis at the collective level.

This shift in focus leads to my conclusion. I have argued that socio-cultural elements residing in Icelandic culture were, combined with global expertise, instrumental in building the core of the successful Icelandic national teams in recent years. Based on this argument, it is important to account for various social influences and different social contexts, as well as to bear in mind that social phenomena – such as Iceland's sporting success – are not subject to control; that is, they were not the result of a carefully organized, linear, long-term plan that was aimed at this goal. This fact makes nations' collective achievement unpredictable and intriguing, as there is no way to see such collective achievements coming; moreover, there is no guarantee that copying the methods from one community to the next will prove to be successful. The secret of Icelandic sports is that there is no secret. The characteristics of the Icelandic national teams, which are present in all the aforementioned teams, are embedded in the local national culture but also affected by global influences. The players perceive this as the norm of doing things and to which they are accustomed. This is highlighted in how Icelanders play and approach sport. The dynamic interplay of various cultural components in recent years has created a sports culture that at present is well suited for Iceland to make its mark in international sport – and Iceland has done well to utilize the opportunities that have risen. This culture is dynamic, where many important elements are coming together at the same time. Thus, with the constant development of sport in society, both at the local and global level, Iceland's remarkable sporting successes that we have witnessed in recent years may not last. Pessimists would argue that when those social components will become unfavorable the Icelandic teams could disappear from the top-level international sport scene as swiftly as they emerged on it. Optimists would on the other hand argue that with the added international experience and expertise, which Icelandic sports have gained in recent years, the success of Icelandic teams will continue. Only time will tell; I suspect however that the reality will be something in between.

Notes

1 Field notes from my visits to Denmark and Holland.
2 See: https://panamapapers.icij.org
3 "Aldagömul pólitísk og viðskiptaleg spilling" (article; *Frettatiminn.is.*, 2016, April). See: www.frettatiminn.is/aldagomul-politisk-og-vidskiptaleg-spilling/
4 See coverage on growing doping of Kenyan athletes: "Athletics-Kenya acknowledges growing doping problem" (article; *Reuters.com.*, 2013, August). See: www.reuters.com/article/us-athletics-kenya-drugs-idUSBRE97902B20130810. See on the decline of Norwegian men's football: Telseth, F. and Halldorsson, V. (forthcoming, "Size need not matter," to be published in a special issue of *Sport in Society*, Sept/Oct 2017).
5 "Framlög til ísí fjórfölduð" (article; *Mbl.is.*, 2016, July). See: www.mbl.is/sport/frettir/2016/07/28/framlog_til_isi_fjorfoldud/

134 *How it all comes together*

References

Ankersen, R. (2012). *The gold mine effect: Crack the secretes of high performance.* London: Ikon.

Chambliss, D.F. (1988). *Champions: The making of Olympic swimmers.* New York: William Morrow.

Coleman, J. (1988). Social capital in the creation of human capital. *American Journal of Sociology,* 94: 95–120.

Collins, T. (2013). *Sport in capitalist society: A short history.* London: Routledge.

Durrenberger, E.P., and Palsson, G. (eds.) (2015). *Gambling debt: Iceland's rise and fall in the global economy.* Boulder: University Press of Colorado.

Goffman, E. ([1967]/2008). *Interaction ritual: Essays on face-to-face behavior.* New York: Anchor Books.

Harper, D. (1987). *Working knowledge: Skill and community in a small shop.* Chicago: The University of Chicago Press.

Hofstede, G., Hofstede, G.J. and Minkov, M. (2010). *Cultures and organizations, software of the mind: Intercultural cooperation and its importance for survival.* New York: McGraw-Hill.

Huizinga, J. ([1938]/1971). *Homo ludens: A study of the play-element in culture.* London: Paladin.

Mills, C.W. ([1951]/2002). *White collar: The American middle classes.* Oxford: Oxford University Press.

Mixa, M.W. and Vaiman, V. (2015). Individualistic Vikings: Culture, economics and Iceland. *Icelandic Review of Politics and Administration,* 11(2): 355–374.

Obermayer, B. and Obermaier, F. (2016). *The Panama papers: Breaking the story of how the rich & powerful hide their money.* London: OneWorld.

Peterson, T. (2008). The professionalization of sport in the Scandinavian countries. *Idrottsforum.* Available online at: www.idrottsforum.org/articles/peterson/peterson 080220.html.

Sennett, R. (2008). *The craftsman.* New Haven: Yale University Press.

Thorlindsson, T. (2011). Bring in the social context: Towards an integrated approach to health promotion and prevention. *Scandinavian Journal of Public Health,* 39(6): 19–25.

Veblen, T. ([1899]/1970). *The theory of the leisure class: An economic study of institutions.* London Unwin.

Veblen, T. ([1915]/1964). *Imperial Germany and the industrial revolution.* New York: Augustus M. Kelley.

Wieting, S. (2015). *The sociology of hypocrisy: An analysis of sport and religion.* London: Routledge.

Appendix

Table A.1 Semi-structured interviews (N=39)

Time of interview	Name	Gender	Year of birth	Nationality	Occupational status*
Spring 2014	Ása Inga Þorsteinsdóttir	F	1982	Iceland	National team coach (women's team gymnastics)
Spring 2014	Íris Mist Magnúsdóttir	F	1987	Iceland	National team player (women's team gymnastics)
12.01 2016	Richard Tahtinen	M	1981	Finland	Former national team coach (men's ice hockey)
13.01 2016	Finnur Freyr Stefánsson	M	1983	Iceland	Assistant national team coach (men's basketball)
01.02 2016	Steinar J. Lúðvíksson	M	1941	Iceland	Historian and former sport journalist
15.01 2016	Ingi Þór Steinþórsson	M	1972	Iceland	Basketball coach (men's, women's club and youth national teams)
18.01 2016	Heimir Hallgrímsson	M	1967	Iceland	National team coach (men's football)
23.01 2016	Líney Halldórsdóttir	F	1961	Iceland	Secretary-General of the Icelandic National Sport and Olympic Association (ISI)
04.02 2016	Sigurður Ragnar Eyjólfsson	M	1973	Iceland	National team coach (women's football) and technical director/coach education director of the Icelandic Football Association (KSI)
05.02 2016	Þorgrímur Þráinsson	M	1959	Iceland	Former national team player and current member of the national team's staff (men's football)
10.02 2016	Ólafur Stefánsson	M	1973	Iceland	National team player, assistant national team coach, coach of the u21 team (men's handball)
11.02 2016	Björgvin Páll Gústafsson	M	1985	Iceland	National team player (men's handball)
11.02 2016	Einar Örn Jónsson	M	1975	Iceland	Sport broadcaster at RUV (The Icelandic National Broadcasting Service) and former national team player (men's handball)
19.02 2016	Guðjón Guðmundsson	M	1954	Iceland	Sport broadcaster at Stöð 2 (Channel 2) and former staff member of the national team (men's handball)
23.02 2016	Patrekur Jóhannesson	M	1972	Iceland	Former national team member (men's handball) and current national team coach (men's handball team of Austria)

Date	Name		Year	Country	Description
25.02 2016	Eggert Magnússon	M	1947	Iceland	Former president of the Icelandic National Football Association and former Chairman of Stoke City FC and West Ham Utd FC
11.03 2016	Hermundur Sigmundsson	M	1964	Iceland	Former handball player and current Associate Professor in the department of Psychology at the Norwegian University of Science and Technology, Norway
16.03 2016	Lars Lagerbäck	M	1948	Sweden	National team coach (men's football)
17.03 2016	Gunnleifur Gunnleifsson	M	1975	Iceland	National team player (men's football)
21.03 2016	Auður Inga Þorsteinsdóttir	F	1978	Iceland	General secretary of the Icelandic Youth Association (UMFÍ) and of Gerpla (women's gymnastics team)
21.03 2016	Anna Úrsúla Guðmundsdóttir	F	1985	Iceland	National team player (women's handball)
05.04 2016	Klara Bjartmarz	F	1969	Iceland	General secretary of the Icelandic Football Association (KSÍ)
07.04 2016	Carsten V. Jensen	M	1963	Denmark	Head of sport (men's football team of FC Nordsjylland Denmark)
10.04 2016	Darren Lough	M	1989	England	Professional football player (in Iceland)
11.04 2016	Craig Pedersen	M	1966	Canada	National team coach (men's basketball)
14.04 2016	Úlfar Hinriksson	M	1972	Iceland	Youth football coach (men's, women's club teams and youth national teams)
18.04 2016	Margrét Lára Viðarsdóttir	F	1986	Iceland	National team player (women's football)
18.04 2016	Hlynur Bæringsson	M	1982	Iceland	National team player (men's basketball)
19.04 2016	Guðmundur Þórður Guðmundsson	M	1960	Iceland	National team coach (Icelandic and Danish men's handball teams)
20.14 2016	Magnús Agnar Magnússon	M	1974	Iceland	Football agent at Total Football
21.04 2016	Rini de Groot	M	1955	Holland	Head youth scouting (men's football team of PSV Eindhoven, Holland)

(Continued)

Table A.1 (Continued)

Time of interview	Name	Gender	Year of birth	Nationality	Occupational status*
21.04 2016	Bart Heuvingh	M	1989	Holland	Youth Academy coach (men's football team of AZ Alkmaar, Holland)
22.04 2016	Jörg Jacobs	M	1970	Germany	Director of sport (men's football team of FC Cologne, Germany)
28.04 2016	Ari Freyr Skúlason	M	1987	Iceland	National team player (men's football)
29.04 2016	Alfreð Finnbogason	M	1989	Iceland	National team player (men's football)
02.05 2016	Þorgerður Katrín Gunnarsdóttir	F	1965	Iceland	Former Minister of Education, Science and Culture (and sport).
12.07 2016	Anton Bjarnason	M	1947	Iceland	Former national team player (football, basketball, volleyball), PE teacher and lecturer at Iceland University of Education
28.09 2016	Júlíus Jónasson	M	1964	Iceland	National team coach (women's handball) and former national team player (men's handball)
29.09 2016	Jón Arnór Stefánsson	M	1982	Iceland	National team player (basketball)

* Occupational status relevant to the timespan of the case in question. Some of the interviewees have changed jobs since then.

Index

ability based groups 84
affluence 26, 28, 34
Age of Settlement 25–6
Akbachev, Boris 45–6
altruistic behavior 80–1
amateur ethos *see* amateurism
amateurism 9, 33–5, 48–9, 55, 62, 67,
    99–103, 106, 127–8, 131; amateur
    ethos 3, 33, 45, 61, 95–8, 100, 127,
    131
anonymity 106, 130
Archetti, Eduardo 75–7, 114–15

basketball 5, 9, 43, 67, 108; amateur
    status 99, 102, 132; coaching
    46–7; competitions 6–9, 34, 49,
    55, 57; disadvantages 5, 34–5, 71;
    organization 34, 50–1; participation
    31–2; spirit 71–2, 74, 76, 80–6, 89,
    109, 117–18; unorthodox play 88–9
Becker, Howard S. 18–20, 65, 73
blood relations 107–8
bonus payments 35, 131
Bosman case 48

Cerulo, Karen 84, 86–7
Champions League 8
character 65–77, 87, 96, 126–30;
    character contest 73–5; dual
    character 83–5, 127–8
character contest *see* character
chess 16, 114
Chihuahua dogs 71
"Cinderella story" 4

closed skilled sports *see* skills
coaching 15, 57–9, 61, 72, 76, 79, 81,
    84–9, 98, 102–20, 111–12, 126;
    foreign coaches 44–7, 101–20; as
    work 29–30, 33–4, 42–3; prestige
    7, 52
collectivism 83, 86, 127; communal
    relations 83–4, 86–7, 127–8
commercialization 3–4, 95, 99, 128,
    130–1
communal relations *see* collectivism
competitive play 96–7
conspicuous consumption 129
craftsmanship 50, 89, 98
culture 11, 17–18, 20–1, 25, 27, 60,
    65, 67–9, 83–4, 102, 107, 109,
    125–6, 129, 133; "ideoculture" 18,
    54–6; sport culture 10, 29, 41, 45,
    101, 111, 128, 130, 133; team culture
    47, 53–5, 81
cultural production 17
cultural toolkits 41–2

"dehumanization" 96
deliberate practice 15, 86
"delinquent gang" 68
disadvantage 5, 68–9, 71, 87, 89, 106
dual character *see* character

economic boom 14
economic crash 14, 56–7
egoists 56, 83–7, 118, 128
Einarsson, Vilhjálmur 28
elder-brother complex 59–60, 115